Sounds of Glory

Volume Two
The Punk and Ska Years

Garry Bushell

NEW HAVEN PUBLISHING LTD UK

First Edition
Published 2016
NEW HAVEN PUBLISHING LTD
www.newhavenpublishingltd.com
newhavenpublishing@gmail.com

Cover design©Pete Cunliffe
pcunliffe@blueyonder.co.uk

newhaven
publishing

Acknowledgements

This book is a compilation of articles from two previous collections. I'd like to thank everyone who helped make it possible. Big love too to Tania and my family: Julie, Danny, Robert, Jenna and Ciara.

Content

Introduction

In 1978, I lucked my way into a staff job on the rock weekly Sounds. NME said punk was dead, but I was going out and seeing great bands every week – the Ruts, the Skids, the UK Subs, the Members and later the Angelic Upstarts and the Cockney Rejects. It was a magical time. I saw the Specials play their very first gig as the Specials supporting the Clash in Aylesbury. That was my first review in the paper!

When the Mod revival started, I was there; and I was there for the birth pangs of the New Wave of British Heavy Metal too (see Volume One of these memoirs).

Even to write these opening words unlocks a flood of memories: getting tongue-tied when I met Joe Strummer, going on the road with The Jam and on a demo with Tom Robinson, becoming mates with Jimmy Pursey, eating pizza with U2, reviewing their demo tape, writing the 2Tone magazine Dance Craze, compiling the Oi albums, being mesmerised by Debbie Harry, being bamboozled into managing the Cockney Rejects, getting rat-arsed with The Blood...many, many times. Life is a drink and you get drunk when you're young..

For six years I had the best job in the world, then like a fool I walked away from it. For the next three decades I've had people asking me about those glory days. What was Weller like? Is Ozzy really nuts? What crazy conspiracy kept the Gonads out of the charts...?

You can't put your arms around your memories, but you can sure as hell write a book about 'em. These were the best years of my life. I hope you enjoy them.

RUDE BOYS CAN'T FAIL
The Specials

New York, March 1980

WOW. New York, just like I pictured it. Skyscrapers n' everything...it's my first time in Manhattan as an adult and I'm up early soaking up the grandeur of the great Babylon, those huge triumphant buildings standing proud against the heraldic blue of the sky. This is the greatest city in the world, for now at least: vibrant, can-do, aggressive and magnificent; a chest-beating, cock-waving monument to all-conquering capitalism; a "fuck you" middle finger salute to the world that can't quite disguise the fact that all of this fancy architecture is just a jog away from heart-breaking poverty. There's a bag-lady on the corner below, and we're a handful of blocks down the street from slums, muggers and junkie slime. In the midst of plenty...

"Oi Garry, you can't have a piss there!" A rowdy Midlands accent rudely disrupts my meditations. I glance around to see a rogues' gallery of reprobates getting snapped for posterity by my infamous sidekick, Ross Halfin, the photographer known to Sounds readers as Gross Halfwit. We're one floor up the concrete colossus that is the World Trade Centre and the paunchy out-of-town Yanks wombling past don't quite know how to take this disrespectful mob of uncouth Limeys who are cavorting and clowning around for a camera instead of paying homage to NYC's breath-taking self-confidence.

The Specials, for it is they, are an odd-looking bunch: two quiet white guys in chunky all-American cardigans, a black bloke in a woollen hat, another black fella in a Gl helmet and army green bomber jacket, a lairy-looking geezer in a tatty sheepskin, a 20-year-old in a white Harrington jacket and green tartan trousers with the staring eyes of a paralysed owl, and, strangest of all a yobbish chancer with no front teeth sporting DM boots, a soccer scarf and donkey jacket, who is much prone to making many strange ejaculations: "Gorblimey", he says. "On ya bike", "I'm fed up with all this homosexual phallic imagery", and so on. It's like a form of football terrace Tourette's.

7

Above our heads, obscuring half a wall is a gigantic tapestry that looks like an Arab sheik's front room rug with a bad case of mumps. Donkey-jacket guy's chubby face breaks out in a huge cherubic grin. "'Ere, let's do one with this carpet," he hollers, and a respectable tourist behind me starts to tut loudly as the cheery hooligans form a painful looking human pyramid in order for him to swing on the mounted monstrosity.

"It's the closest you'll get to a good shag," remarks Halfin to a chorus of laughs and abuse. "2-Tone band in 'hard rugs' scandal," was the best I could come up with.

'Hey, stop your messing around/Better think of your future/Time you straighten right out/Creating problems in town...' Outraged of suburbia doesn't realise that he is tutting the driving force behind the hottest pop phenomenon of the moment, that this funny-looking fella with the missing front teeth is on the way to fulfilling a dream that he's been pursuing since his mid-teens.

JEREMY David Hounsell Dammers, known to a grateful world as Jerry, is not your run-of-the-mill pop star. Dammers is different, complicated. Some might say weird. A shy guy, he finds it hard to talk with people he doesn't know and on first meeting you could easily assume some village had lost its idiot. Unusually for someone in his position, Jerry isn't at all self-centred, and he nurtures an almost obsessive hatred of elitism, privilege and waste – the cornerstones of this marvellous little industry we call Pop with its legions of plastics, pretenders, parasites, preening popinjays and budding Hitlers. People who know him say his ambition isn't for himself but for his music, his dream...

Born in India, Jerry Dammers grew up mostly in the Midlands. His dad was a vicar, not particularly rich or poor, and he spent his teen years rebelling against his family background of restrictive Sunday righteousness. He'd drink too much, smash things up, run away from home - anything to get up his parents' hooters, to be different from them.

Most importantly, he got into music. The Who, The Kinks, the Small Faces, Otis Redding and Tamla Motown were his first loves, along with the joyous bliss of Trojan reggae. Even as young as 15, almost a decade ago, Dammers had the idea of merging rock and reggae together "although no-one in rock circles took reggae seriously back then." Over the years, four of which were spent in the pursuit of a fine art diploma, he slogged away in various pub and club bands trying to get them to play his songs with little success.

The Sex Pistols kicked open the door for a whole generation. And the idea, until then expressed only on home demo tapes made with the Selecter's Neol Davies, crystallized into something more than a dream. Exhibiting an almost frightening single-mindedness, Dammers built up the people around him who became the Specials by way of the Coventry Automatics. An odd bunch: two authentic rude boys (Neville and Lynval), two grammar school boys (Jerry and Horace), rocker (Roddy) and a punk (Terry).

THE SPECIALS made their debut at Aylesbury in July 1978 as a five piece. By pure chance, I was there doing my first ever review for Sounds and I wrote 'Whereas the Clash play punk songs and reggae songs, the Specials combine elements of the two. Yeah it sounds a phoney not to say disjointed formula but surprise, surprise, it worked.' Move over Nostradamus, you've just lost your crown...

Of course I had no idea just how well it would work. The dream was still embryonic then and thanks to Bernie Rhodes that tour was the last we saw of the band till March '79 when a then-sane Dave McCullough rediscovered them and wrote the first-ever feature on the band. By then they were the real thing. Not just a working idea but a whole new music, a punky-reggae party – punk in feel and bite, Ska in the beat. The punk made danceable, the Ska intensified. The message: 2-Tone.

The history you know. They finally gave Rhodes the old Spanish archer and their delicious DIY debut single 'Gangsters', on their own 2-Tone label, kissed him goodbye while cruising up the charts. 'Gangsters' was a re-working of Prince Buster's 1964 smash 'Al Capone', with lyrics taking their old manager to task: "Bernie Rhodes knows, don't argue!" The b-side was 'The Selecter' by the Selecter - Neol Davies and Ray Bradbury, with the trombone solo played, I'm told, by their local newsagent.

The Specials linked arms with PR man turned manager Rick Rogers and his Trigger crew and stood firm against a maelstrom of tempting record company offers until they got the deal they wanted from Chrysalis, a deal to make a dream come true with a surprising degree of autonomy to release what they wanted and sign who they wanted to their own label. Chrysalis cried all the way to the bank.

To date all of the 2-Tone releases have been Top Twenty hits, the Specials had three of them including the first 2-Tone number one with the Special AKA Live ep in January. Their debut album was released in October 1979 and has shifted a cool quarter of a million 'units' to date. The Specials have become more than a band; they're the ringleaders of a movement, the inspiration for a teenage fashion wave, and a brand new dance.

JANUARY 1980 and the band hit America. Hard. Now it's the beginning of March and they've toured for five weeks solid giving the Police a good run for their money on a few dates but mostly headlining, sometimes playing an exhausting two gigs per night, and if you've seen the way they play you'll know what I mean by exhausting. Like at home, they've concentrated on small non-seated venues; the critics have wet themselves and the small part of America that's seen them has loved every bluebeat-backboned minute.

(One step) beyond the live shows, other developments are looking promising too. The album, repackaged Stateside to include 'Gangsters', was released in January and has sold around 100,000 to date, reaching No 80 in the Billboard chart, itself virtually unheard of without a hit single (both Elvis Costello and the Police for example had hits before comparable album success).

Of course the majority of US kids are still in to disco or downers and wine at stadium concerts. But maybe the time is right psychologically for significant numbers of them to break away from the dominant dope culture that's held millions in its dozy grip for over a decade now.

After all, psychologically America is getting a good shake up thanks to the Ayatollah - caricatures of the Iranian counter-revolutionary nuisance, as twisted as any British Movement sticker of Asians, adorn New York. Maybe they'll be jolted out of their complacency. Either way, young America needs a music that doesn't sound tailor-made for lifts or funeral parlours.

'New Wave' is currently the hip craze in the States and the Clash in particular look set to clean up. The times, or at least the charts, could well be a-changing. The usual 'informed rock commentators' didn't think the Specials would do as well as they have here. Which kind of made sense: who would have thoughts the Sherman Tanks would buy into their spirited mix of skinhead moonstomp and puritanical socialism? The big question now is: will the band carry on growing or run out of steam? The irresistible super-pop force of 2-Tone is meeting the immovable object of North American apathy head-on, and it's hard to tell what will happen.

Rude boy singer Neville Staple (born Neville Eugenton Staple according to his passport, in Manchester, Jamaica) is keener on commenting on the women here, and the madness of New York cabbies. "It's like, 'if you don't like the way I drive, stay off the pavement...'" he laughs. But the band admits that financially the whole enterprise has lost around $50,000 to date – probably a conservative estimate – although that's got to be counterbalanced by album sales.

And the tour is obviously an investment for the future. Chrysalis Records clearly believe they could be on to millions which explains why the label's big brass executives are over from England for the last dates. The Specials ain't so sure.

"People are gonna ask us how the American tour went," says lanky bassist Sir Horace Gentleman (né Panter). "And I won't know, there doesn't seem to be any way of gauging it."

"It's been like gig-sleep-get up-travel-gig-sleep non-stop," owl-eyed Terry Hall affirms. "And most of the time playing two gigs a night – it's hard to make much sense of it. Personally I don't think 2-Tone will be as popular over here as it is in England. Fashions don't tend to catch on in a big way over here, the country's too big."

Most of the band has enjoyed the States as an experience although for the black members especially the tour has opened their eyes to a few of the harsher realities behind the US liberal dream, as Lynval Golding (woollen hat and Ska guitar) testifies.

Shaking his head, Jamaican-born Lynval tells me how he'd "walked into this shop in Chicago to buy a watch for my sister, me and Rex our roadie, and the guy says, 'Hey, you can't come in here.' I said 'What's the matter with you?' and as soon as he heard our accents it was 'Can I help you, sir?' I told him to stick his shop up his arse. Can you imagine how they treat American blacks in that state? Another time I was in this bar in Boston wearing a green hat, and this guy turned round with his mate and said 'I like that hat – only trouble is I don't like it on you'."

It's the same the whole world over – and that doesn't make it all right.

As the gruelling tour progressed, tempers frayed and incidents like that helped to keep the band together; that and the inevitable tour anecdotes. Like veteran trombonist Rico sitting up all night hiding his dope in his bible before going through Canadian Customs and then getting busted for smuggling oranges (even though he'd brought them over from the States days before).

In LA, they played eight shows in four days at the Whisky-A-Go-Go. Roddy recalls sitting in the dressing room after the last gig dripping in sweat to find a bunch of supercilious record company 'suits' waiting for them. "I love that song of yours," said one, "'On My Radio'" (by the Selecter!); another asked if they could teach him to pogo. "They wanted us to put our stage clothes back on and pose with them for a photo," he calls. "Jerry, who was really tired, just told them all to 'Fuck off!"

Asked how he liked America, Dammers told the LA Times that he'd had more fun on a school trip to Russia. On another occasion, Jerry was called down to do a breakfast interview in New Orleans after a night on the tiles. Always unpredictable he got up without warning, walked out the hotel and straight into the swimming pool – fully clothed.

'Call me immature, call me a poser/I'd love to spread manure in your bed of roses/Don't wanna be rich, don't wanna be famous/I'd really hate to have the same name as you...'

When I first see him he's in the lift of New York's Hotel Diplomat and he looks like he's spent the last three hours listening to Public Image on an empty stomach. Like drained, mannn. This and tonight's gig do little to dispel my fears that maybe the tail end of the tour wasn't the wisest of times to come over...

THE DIPLOMAT could well have inspired the band's 'Nite Klub', very is-this-the-in-place-to-be, and what am I doing here? Mick Jagger, David Bowie and Debbie Harry from Blondie all turn up tonight – cordoned off from the swinish multitude of course, but even the punters seem more hoighty-toighty than hoi polloi: the place seems to be crawling with trendies and posers who've willingly coughed up the rip-off five quid ticket price (thanks to big time promoter Ron Delsener who gets 'Gangsters' dedicated all to himself) to be seen. It wasn't exactly a bad performance, I've never seen the Specials play badly, but it was a bit lacklustre. They were obviously cream-crackered and there was no magic there, though this didn't stop the crowd going seriously barmy and demanding no less than three encores, last one being an extended version of Rico's instrumental 'Man From Wareika'.

Even below par, the Specials, Debbie tells me later are "at least twice as energetic" as the average New York club band. Personally 'I wouldn't dance in a place like this; it's all a drag and the beer tastes just like piss...' crossed with anti-freeze.

The only thing that made the evening swing for me was meeting a party of Coventry rudies – Evo, Adam, Liam and Dennis; factory worker fans who've spent their holiday pennies coming over to see the Specials (and have had their hotel room paid for by the band as a return gesture). And even more surprising, errant Cockney Rejects fans Bovril Bob, Woolwich Mark and Paul Bradley who were over from London with the Jam; Weller and co were here too with Polydor A&R man and Charlton renegade Dennis Munday.

I went out on the piss with the chaps who were giving it the old "Oily rag, spam" rhyming slang palaver to all-comers as they got increasingly Brahms and Listz. But you can drink anywhere, how often will a tosspot like me see Manhattan? I discreetly slipped off to see the sights on me Todd. Big city, New York, bright lights, sure looks pretty, but believe me this time of night, in this weather, half-cut and on your Jack the Big Apple's more like a Granny Smith nipped by an early frost.

Back in the hotel room, though, I stare out the window at the Empire State and the Chrysler Building, and the sea of activity on the streets below, a world of corner delis, delivery men and doormen...as alien to the English visitor accustomed to UK licensing laws as the deep-fired knish the street vendors sell. New York, New York...so good they named it like a sitcom amnesiac; God's gift to grateful insomniacs.

That whole city that never sleeps thing is as true as the song tells you. A stark contrast to Milton Keynes, the city where there's nothing to get up for...Or Middlesbrough, the city that just gets pissed and shits the bed.

NEXT DAY was the photo session and also the first time I'd really sat down for a proper chinwag with the band who are nowhere near as mean moody and difficult as their stage image might suggest. Terry in particular was an easy-going revelation. I'd spoken to Jerry Dammers a few times before but only by telephone and that has always been easier because on the phone at his cluttered little flat in Coventry with his art school paintings on the wall and the postcard of Ken Dodd on the fireplace, he can be his real single-minded self, very concerned and finicky. In the flesh it's harder and he's obviously happier taking the piss out of the lovely Horace, picking up matchsticks and talking to them as if they were the lanky bassist.

No matter. Band philosophy has it that in no way is Jerry any sort of leader/spokesman. He'd probably string you up for suggesting it. They insist that the Specials are very much equal partners. Jerry is just the one who made it happen, the one who had the dream first of all, and believe me the dream is catching.

Back in England the dream has come in for some battering lately, mostly from Sounds resident reggae expert Eric Fuller whose comments have given the impression that 2-Tone represents the biggest carve-up since the Lord Mayor's Banquet. Fuller basically accused the band of ripping off Jamaican artists by half-inching their original songs. Those initial broadsides seem to have unleashed a veritable orgy of anti-2-Tone feeling in the rock press. This week for example 2-Tone is variously "boring" (the scathing

Melody Maker), "the rotting undergrowth of Ska" (NME), and "sickly exploitative Ska" (Sounds).

Strangely enough all the peddlers of trite, rehashed head music and elitist, completely ineffective 'radicalism', feel threatened by this morally impeccable dance music. Surely not because it's got through to ordinary kids, instead of sticking safely in University seminar rooms, and actually created a whole new ball game for hundreds of thousands of teenagers?

Still the Grim Brigade draw up their battle lines and the Ska boys don't give a monkey's toss: 'If you don't like it you don't have to dance'. These self-styled intellectuals are as out to lunch as a gluttonous fat cat with a no-limit expense account. In April last year one of their number described the Specials thus, 'dance music with a vengeance...the very finest pop songs...fresh and new and paradoxically familiar', and made reference to the 'sheer integrity of Dammer's terribly effective lyrics'. What's changed? Success! The Specials crime has been to sign to a major company (while adamantly retaining their integrity), to become popular and to have Effectively Communicated. How damning! How pathetic...

LYNVAL Golding takes Eric Fuller's assertions to heart. "What amazes me about the whole thing is that Jerry has just got to be about the fairest person on earth," he tells me. "I've known him for years and if there's even a half pence discrepancy with money he ain't happy, it all has to be shared. Jerry has got no interest in money, none at all. When we put in the musical quotations from classic Ska songs like 'Too Much Too Young' and the others, he tried to make sure the money would get to the right person, cos in Jamaica everyone ripped off everyone but he'd keep on trying to find the real writer. As long as he's got his music, food and a place to eat Jerry's happy."

'I don't wanna be rich/Don't wanna be famous/I wouldn't wanna have the same name as you!'

Lynval talks about Rico Rodriguez, who played trombone on the original of 'Rudy, A Message To You' and Prince Buster numbers like 'Barrister Pardon' and who along with flugelhorn player Dick Cluthell has accompanied the Specials on this tour and their last UK one. "We could be paying him a session fee but he gets the same as all of us and we're gonna bring his next album out on 2-Tone. Rico will tell you about Prince Buster and the way HE used to rip everyone off and how in the end no one would play with him. The reason Rico's stuck with us so long is that we've treated him fair and he's never been treated like that before."

Sadly I missed my chance to speak with Rico. There was a bit of trouble at Liberty Island, and then the band had to shoot off to Long Island for a sound check. I didn't get there until hours later, but for once I arrived in style...

I am far too punk and bolshy to be star-struck but I will admit that as I was being driven in a huge black Lincoln stretch limo over the Brooklyn Bridge at sunset with Debbie Harry, the most beautiful woman in pop, sitting opposite me, her eyes so blue they made the Med seem murky, Chris Stein chopping out lines of cocaine and a magnum bottle of champagne on ice sitting in the corner, there was a fair bit of pinching myself going on, along with the recurring thought: wait till I tell 'em about this in the Swan in Charlton Village. (Sell out! – Ed). This was the only time this weekend I really couldn't believe I was here...

Chris played us tapes of new New York rappers along with vintage Prince Buster songs and raved about the previous night's crowd. "The New York audience never gets like that except for the first twenty rows," he affirmed excitedly. But that night's gig at Speaks Club was even better. It wasn't supposed to be at Speaks, it was supposed to be at My Father's Place, but they couldn't cope with the ticket design.

BACKSTAGE, the dressing room is over-run with rowdy rudies and band members, with old Rico with his dope watching through his slit-like eyes, and Dammers as ever collapsed in a corner snoring like a contented wart-hog. The band's laudably open attitude to having people in the dressing room stems largely from their experiences on the Clash tour in 1978, when everyone was kicked out when Strummer and the boys were on stage and not allowed to scoff the food – the Specials had to hide in cupboards just to be able to get at something to eat.

I get Terry Hall, former clerical worker at a Coventry stamp and coin dealers, into a corner for a quick bunny about the future. The man the bungling LA Times called an 'energetic Jamaican' looks and sounds suspiciously English to these non-specialist eyes and he laughs much more than you'd have thought. Seems the band are having one week off (apart from Xmas their first since September), then there's a one-off Paris gig, sort of a 2-Tone works outing, and then they're in the studio to lay down a few tracks from which a single will come although the boys are adamant that they won't be rushed.

Possible next number ones are Roddy Radiation's 'Rat Race' and Lynval and Neville Staple's autobiographical 'Rude Boys Out Of Jail' (Staple, the man behind the introduction of most of the 'musical quotations', in the Special's songs, did a sentence for burglary, affray and driving getaway cars before his current occupation as MC/vocalist and feels strongly about getting the 'prison is no fun' message across to potential villains in the crowd).

Possible future signings for 2-Tone are the Swinging Cats from Coventry featuring Jerry's girlfriend (Terry calls them "three brothers and an auntie") and from LA an all-girl sixties style New Wave pop band with punk roots called the Go-Gos who might be supporting the Specials here in the UK soon. Then there's Rico's album, and Desmond Dekker has submitted a tape for consideration – 2-Tone's about ripping off blacks, can't you see?

Apparently all the band have got new songs, Lynval wants to do his own album, drummer John Bradbury has a version of Rex Garvin And The Mighty Cravers 'Sock It To 'Em JB' out some time (the only reason for the whispered new Specials 'soul' direction it would appear). There is also an idea for Neville and Madness's Chas Smash to do a one-off single with Nev as Judge Roughneck trying Chas for dancing too mechanically...And in the longer term there are dreams of launching their own recording studio, opening a club in Coventry, and generally building 2-Tone as the Tamla or Stax of our generation.

"We just want to make sure it stays a natural process," says Terry. "And not get pushed in directions we don't want to go in. It may seem to have happened fast to you but really it's the culmination of years of having nothing. We're not exactly rich now; the royalties won't come through till later next year. But we wanna keep ploughing money back, which doesn't mean we're gonna go round saying we're gonna help Tom, Dick and Harry, but we will be an alternative for people who deserve the help and who want to use us."

MAYBE AN hour later Debbie Harry walks on stage like a vision and announces the band, and then Terry Hall adopts his Son of Rotten glowering stage persona to lead them on. At their first US gig he caustically announced "This is it, my little petals, this is your last chance to dance before World War III" – so near the knuckle. Tonight it's a sarky "This is our last show in America – you must have enjoyed every minute of us."

Hall comes across as a kind of depressed Dracula, with those big, burning eyes, deathly pale face and that alternatively hung-up and hang-dog expression. And he sings Dammers's sometimes funny, sometimes acidic words with a barbed bitterness. At times he dances on the spot, but mostly he's static, looking like the eye of a hurricane with his compatriots a whirling powerhouse behind him, especially the ultra-athletic Neville who hurtles around the stage, balancing on speakers, be it sporting either a smart 2-Tone whistle or dressed up to the nines as Judge Roughneck or later stripped down to natty briefs as it gets TOO hot. (And he wants to show the girls what he's got...)

Guitarists Lynval and Roddy do their lesser runs (Rod sometimes going through the complete set of Paul Simonon classic poses) while Horace moves gracefully, dancing with his bass held high. Then there's Brad at the back, a rock solid anchor man (no nautical implications, JB), his drumming as aggressive and self-assured as the man himself. And finally, there's Mister Jekyll & Hyde, Jerry Dammers. Put him behind his organ in front of an audience and all that off-stage uneasiness dissolves. We're left with an animated madman pounding away for dear life because his dream depends on it.

At one stage tonight he leaves his keyboards and just collapses on stage lying motionless till the near-naked Neville descends on him and perches on his back, and Dammers lifts his head to reveal a grin as wide as the Hudson River, the grin of a man totally content and gloriously optimistic.

It wouldn't be enough to say they were good tonight. They were brilliant. Tomorrow they were going home and it was like they had to burn up every last drop of adrenalin left in them, amplified as the biggest dance beat around, transforming a rotten sweaty club in to the hottest place on earth with all the old favourites and the two new numbers, both bristling with a typical richness, morality and spiky dance attack, poured out in what even Eric Fuller would surely have deemed a "well iry session".

Of course it ended with a ridiculous number of encores, this time totally deserved. Lynval got so carried away he bounced right off the tiny stage, and at the very end Brad trashed his kit through pure passion. And there was me with a big dopy grin on my boat, thinking this is rock 'n' roll, these boys could be the real heirs to Chuck Berry and John Lee Hooker's thrones, the direct descendant of the glorious violent dance beat of primal R&B, carried across on the airwaves to Jamaica, reinterpreted as Ska, carried on to England, nurtured in bargain bins then finally mated with the white riot of 70s English youth, the whole damn thing making for a passionate dance power that just cuts through all the phoniness, pretentions and corruptions of the contemporary music scene.

The next day I left behind the Lego buildings and lemming-like joggers of New York, secure in the knowledge that the band I'd been with are very special indeed.

Postscript: This account, a version of which was published originally in Sounds in 1980, was accurate but not entirely comprehensive. At the gig, demob crazy on our last night in the USA, Ross and I found ourselves chatted up by two no doubt short-sighted Brooklyn punkettes with accents broader than Central Park. We ended up inviting them back to the hotel. Debbie Harry was disgusted and I was shunted up front with the chauffeur in shame with both of the girls on my lap. This is when Claudia whispered in my ear: "My friend doesn't like your friend..."

Back in Manhattan, we lost Gross, found a dealer, drained the mini-bar and, let's just say that I enjoyed the kind of night that had so far eluded me after they called last orders at the Blackheath & Newbridge Working Men's Club. I've felt nostalgic about New York ever since...

Neville Staple had an unusual day too. A fan came up and gave the band a thank you bag of cocaine – about five grams worth. Nev shot off to the gent's to sample it, and as he was chatting to a fan by the cubicle, a fella with a mop of white hair breezed up and said, "Are you having a toot?" Nev recalled: "I looked up into the face of Andy Warhol...meeting one of the greatest living artists of the 20th Century in a bog in New York. What are the chances of that happening?"

FUCK LAW AND ORDER
The Angelic Upstarts

North East England, April 1979

GERRY the roadie walks on to the stage to hang up the band's banner. It's a Union Jack embellished with the words 'Upstarts Army' and an angry socialist clenched fist. The banner also boasts the uncompromising motto 'Smash Law And Order', and a drawing of a pig in a helmet cruelly entitled 'PC Fuck Pig'. The audience starts to laugh and cheer, as well they might. They're convicts, we're in prison and the punk rock band about to play is the Angelic Upstarts. That's right. THE BAND THE POLICE LOVE TO HATE IS PLAYING A PRISON GIG.

Singer Thomas 'Mensi' Mensforth isn't the only one not sure that we'll get out alive. Or at all. It seems that the prison chaplain, nice fella, reminds me of Mr Barrowclough from the BBC sitcom Porridge, has booked the notorious South Shields punk combo on the strength of their name alone. They're angelic, see; he has yet to discover that this lot are not wholly holy. But then as Voltaire knew you have to have the devil in you to properly succeed in any of the arts.

Mensi is a big lad, with a face straight out of the Beano comic, but right now he looks as worried as the proverbial long-tailed cat in a room full of rocking chairs.

"What's the matter with you man?" asks Keith Bell, the Upstarts' stocky, barrel-chested manager as the gates of HMP Acklington close behind us half an hour earlier. Mensi shakes his big cartoon head and mutters: "They always said I'd end up inside, but I - aa - never thought it'd be like this." Bell laughs and Mensi grins but that's just to hide the fact that he was shitting himself. Who isn't? Only Keith Bell seems completely at ease.

Even now as he prepares to take to the stage, Mensi is fretting. "Hey what if they don't let us out, man?" Keith takes no notice. A self-confessed former gangster, he's been here before – when he stayed a lot longer than we intend to. After visiting his house last night I'm not too convinced about the 'former' part of that previous sentence. The windows of his terraced home are attractively lined with metal grills on account of the fact that someone threw a petrol bomb through a downstairs' one not so long ago. Well, it could happen to anyone.

Bell, a one-time North Eastern Counties light-middleweight boxing champ, maintains order at their gigs on the basis of his reputation alone.

Acklington Prison in Northumbria is less than an hour's drive north from the Upstarts home town of South Shields, Tyne and Wear. It's a Category C men's prison, described to me as a fast-growing semi-open jail, a limbo where men come, like Bell had once come, to finish their sentences, though recently lifers have started to number among Her Majesty's cooped-up clientele.

We stroll across the grounds to meet the poor, unsuspecting Chaplain who outlines some rules and regulations and smiles when Keith asks if he knows they're a punk rock group. He still thinks he's getting Christian rock. So why is it happening? Certainly not for the dosh – the fee doesn't even cover the Upstarts' expenses, and I know them well enough to know that this isn't just a lame publicity stunt. For starters I'm the only one here from the rock press and I invited myself.

This gig, was entirely the band's idea, partly because there was virtually nowhere else left in the North East of England that they could play, and partly as a favour to the men inside, some of whom they knew from the Shields. The Upstarts and their entourage are eleven strong and the inmates are genuinely pleased to see us. The cons testify that this is the first entertainment on offer in Acklington for many a long month. They're grateful and excited. Scores of blokes pack into the tiny hall as soon as the gear's set up, cheering the band through a sound check version of Sham 69's 'Borstal Breakout'. Gigantic geezers of 30-plus who make Meat Loaf look like Tiny Tim wander in with their hair spiked up with Brylcream, unlaced plimsolls (the laces have been removed), and grins as wide as their tattooed, prison gym biceps.

Soon there are about 150 in with a few anxious screws watching from outside. A fella with 'cut here' tattooed across his neck eggs on an ex-busker inmate to jump up and jam with the band in a 12-bar sound check muck about. When roadie Gerry unfurls the stage banner the men laugh out loud and the colour drains entirely from the poor old chaplain's boat race. He couldn't look more shocked if Mensi had produced a small nun from his hold-all and started banging her over the guitar amps.

And I wouldn't put that past him, either.

Still nervous, but hiding it well, Tom Mensforth bowls on to the stage and the band wham-bam into the opening number, 'Police Oppression'.

This has to be the ultimate irony – the Angelic Upstarts, a band who the Northumbria cops view perhaps rightly as being roughly as welcome as Crippen serving mystery cocktails, are guests of HM government for an exercise in subversion.

Rows of lumps with ink that makes my tats look like heat spots watch the stage antics intensely, the younger ones swaying with the beat, the older ones a bit bemused, but all of them clapping a thunderous approval at the end of each song. And the more they enjoy it the more Mensi starts to loosen up, dropping in the odd "My name is Sue, how do you do?" throwbacks to Johnny Cash's pioneering 1969 San Quentin gig, swearing at the mixing desk, stripping his shirt off, spitting at the ceiling (they loved that) and bellowing along like a wounded bison to the raw rock 'n' roll that makes the Upstarts one of the handful of real punk bands left in this fast decaying country.

Everything they do, everything they write, is pickled in the history and attitudes of the North East: ranging from the Jarrow Crusade to the kind of men you might have seen in the film Get Carter. The shipyards, mines and the Labour Party are there, but so, unspoken, are the armed robbers, cat burglars and hard men. Working class and criminal class are entwined into an US to pit against the Them of the authorities and the capitalist robber barons.

"There's crooks everywhere but it's always the wrong ones get nicked," announces Mensi to much applause, introducing 'We Are The People', the band's savage put down of police corruption and social double standards.

"This is one you've got to sing along to," he smiles as the band power-drives into a specially amended version of Sham's 'Borstal Breakout': 'There's Gonna Be An Acklington Breakout'…This one's for all the screws, 'Fuck Off And Leave Me Alone'…" and so on. The poor chaplain looks as if he's praying to be struck down by a heavenly thunder bolt, and even the cons who aren't into the band's primal din are loving the spirit, looking over their shoulders – they always look over their shoulders – and grinning at each other. Never more so than on the emotive set-closing 'Murder of Liddle Towers.'

This was the Upstarts' self-financed first single, about electrician Liddle Towers, an amateur boxer from Birtley, Gateshead, arrested for being drunk and disorderly, who died in suspicious circumstances after a spell in police custody three years ago. Mensi's lyrics leave the listener in no doubt as to whom he blamed for the 39-year-old's untimely death:

'He was beaten black, he was beaten blue/But don't be alarmed, it was the right thing to do/Police have the power, police have the right/To kill a man, and take away his life/Who killed Liddle?/Did you kill Liddle?/Who killed Liddle?/Police killed Liddle Towers....'

And Mensi reinforces his opinion, as he usually does, by subtly unveiling the fresh head of a pig which he leaves gurning from atop the amps. (Normally at a live show, he'd set about it with an axe supplied by a local character called Mad Willie; charming guy, collects stamps and presses wild flowers...)

The prison hall explodes with cheers and whistles as cons leap up and punch the air as the singer presses home his advantage: 'Questions are unanswered/ Policemen scared to talk/ Perhaps they're hiding something/ Will our message get across/ Please tell me why/Did he die?/ Tell me now/ Tell me how...'

An encore is inevitable and the Upstarts slam through 'Acklington Breakout' one more time, before the screws let them know it's time to stop. Some of the inmates wander out on cloud nine, still shouting the chorus while others hang back to chat and thank the band.

"That were great," one young con enthuses to me.

Why do you like them? I ask.

"Cos they're just like us, we can identify with 'em."

It's a sentiment Mensi echoes in reverse when we finally, and thankfully, shamble through the prison gates into cars for home:

"That's what frightens me, it could so easily have been me in there. When I think of some of the things I've - aa've - done...if I wasn't a singer in a band I'd probably be an inmate."

If certain sections of the Northumbria Police get their way he could still be. A few of the prison officers today would have been happier if they'd escorted us from the stage to the cells, and you can't really blame them for that. But instead they let us walk away from the scene of this audacious musical crime. Well, okay, 'walk' isn't the right word. We clear off quicker than a plane load of Nazi Generals high-tailing their way to South America in 1945.

The Upstarts claim that unofficial police activity has left them banned from every club in the North East; there is a long history of personal and group harassments. Northumbria Plod were in the process of charging the band with incitement to violence at the time of the prison gig. "They always get me when I'm by myself, right," spits Mensi. "Two weeks ago I was walking home from my girlfriend's at 4am and this police car pulls up and they start shouting abuse, 'Wanker, fucking poof.' I just ignored them, and they followed us about half a mile down the road at walking distance. Then one of them shouts 'Hey cunt' and I just lost me temper and shouted 'Fuck off'. They jumped out and chased us but I hid in a coal bunker. I went to the police - poliss - inspector and complained the next day and he said 'To tell you the truth son you haven't got a leg to stand on, you've got no witnesses and you've got a criminal record'. Since I've seen him I've had no hassles, mind, but it's only been a week...I'm not anti-poliss. Nobody's got more respect for an honest policeman than I have. You have got to have law and order, but when the poliss become the law, when they start making the law, that's when it's wrong. They're so corrupt up here they can get away with fucking murder."

Mensi gets heated as often as a spinster's kettle, though he doesn't strike me as violent - just strong in his convictions and outraged by what he sees as injustice. But it's easy to see why some feel the need to prove themselves by taking him on and others are outraged by what they feel he stands for.

Appropriately, we get back to Keith Bell's drum to find that the rest of the band have been stopped and interrogated by the police on the way back...An everyday story of South Shields folk.

Mensi, Mond and their on-off drummer Decca Wade grew up together on the Shields' notorious Brockley Whinns council estate; bassist Steve is a 'wetback' from across the Tyne in North Shields, "Steve's posh," Decca liked to joke. "He gets out the bath to have a piss. But where we come from they've got mudguards on the Hoover. They built a youth club on the estate. I wouldn't say it's a dive but Jacques Cousteau is the bouncer..." But then he'd add, more seriously: "We've all lived for 20 years and never even made it to the bottom rung of the ladder yet."

By 1978, the band had notched up forty-three car thefts and ninety-six traffic offences between them. Their other crimes included attempting to break into their local bank by battering in the front door with a house brick. Decca was also arrested for stealing a huge copper boiler with a couple of mates. The cops asked who helped them shift it. "Naybody," Decca replied. The cop's response was "Ye must be bloody bionic."

Uncharitable observers might conclude that maybe police interest in the band's activities weren't quite as unjustified as their lyrics suggest...

The lads' blue collar credentials are impeccable. Decca worked as a "burner" (a welder) in the ship-yards. Mensi had been an apprentice miner down the Westee pit for three and a half years before quitting. It was wet and dangerous work; the coal face was about a mile under the North Sea. "I saw three dead men in my time down there," he says, shaking his head.

The band pissed off a lot of potential fans by wearing swastikas on stage. "To annoy people," Mensi insisted. Well that worked. But good sense prevailed, and that dumb 1977 hang-over has now gone. Tom was, and remains resolutely anti-racist - "We're all black men down the pit," he says, although of course miners can shower. And anti-Nazi: Mensi's first stage shirt was customised with the slogan 'Fascism Kills', and I once saw him head-butt a Geordie who tried to interest him in the National Front in The Ship in Wardour Street. He's just as strongly anti-Tory, too. Not that this prevented the Labour-supporting Daily Mirror from turning the band's prison gig into a front page shock-horror story (headline: Punks Rock A Jailhouse) a few days later and quoting me as "band spokesman", largely because I was the only one they could reach on the phone.

Even funnier, the local Tyneside Tory MP condemned it as "an incredibly stupid thing to allow." His name? Neville Trotter.

An accurate record of the event appeared in the Socialist Worker – I wrote it – quoting the things Mensi had actually told the inmates, like they'd be better off in nick if Mrs Thatcher got elected later this year, and urging punks to vote Labour on the accurate grounds that "Thatcher's Government will destroy the trade union movement." Although you might argue that Scargill was the man who hit the self-destruct button, bringing the unions down with him.

INSPIRED by the Buzzcocks' brilliant Spiral Scratch ep, Mensi and Raymond 'Mond' Cowie formed the Angelic Upstarts in the summer of 1977. Their first gig was arranged for the Civic Hall in neighbouring Jarrow, where they were pelted by the audience with pretty much everything that came to hand. The band's first roadie, Skin Brown, was hit on the head by a table and needed seven stitches. Their original bassist and drummer quit there and then.

Music was Mensi's escape from a life time down the pits. At the time of the Acklington gig he was on £15 a week from the band's new WEA advance – Warners snapped them up after Polydor dropped them like a hot turd when Mensi had a full-on toe-to-toe fist-fight with a security guard, who lost.

Bassist Steve Forsten and the latest drummer Keith 'Sticks' Warrington were on the dole having packed up brick-laying and bakery work respectively at Christmas; and guitarist Mond was still working as a shipyard spark, saying: "I've got to. There's £8 a week to pay in fines for my motoring offences. But I'm packing it in if the single charts."

The single 'I'm An Upstart' peaked at 31, the follow-up 'Teenage Warning' managed 29; and that was as high as they ever got. So Mensi was never really in his dream position of "being in a position where I can say things and be listened to by millions". But he carried on speaking out against racism and capitalism in the music press, while reputedly making a fortune from the used car trade. He was the biggest socialist in Oi, and the only one who ended up minted.

The Upstarts relationship with Keith Bell did not last long. Sacked by the band when he started to knock them about, Bell and his henchmen set about trying to intimidate Upstart fans, even allegedly assaulting people buying their records, before threatening Mensi's mother, smashing her house windows and making threatening and abusive phone calls to her. Reprisal incidents included Mensi and Decca Wade smashing one of the Bell firm's car windows and a midnight visit to Bell's own home by Decca's dad, club comedian Derek Wade and Mensi's brother-in-law Billy Wardropper who blasted one of Bell's henchmen in the leg with a sawn-off shotgun. Hitting back, Bell threatened to kill Wade Senior. Three of his cronies set fire to a stable belonging to Mensi's sister causing almost £5,000 worth of damage. In ensuing court cases both Bell and Billy Wardropper were jailed while Decca's dad copped a year's suspended sentence. Presiding Judge Hall told the Upstarts team: "I accept that all of you suffered a severe amount of provocation, which was none of your seeking. But at the same time I have a duty to condemn the use of firearms, particularly a sawn-off shotgun."

The Upstarts' recorded their opinion in a song called 'Shotgun Solution': 'Shotgun blasts ring in my ears/Shoot some scum who live by fear/A lot of good men will do some time/For a fucking cunt without a spine'

A Fairy Tale Of New York June 1982

Fast forward three years and I'm in Manhattan with the Angelic Upstarts, words I thought I'd never write. To our endless amusement, the Septics – septic tanks, Yanks – all mistake me and Mensi for Australians; me because of my accent, Tom because he looks like a convict fresh off the boat at Botany Bay. In a hurry to get to Tim Sommer's punk/oi radio show, we manage to get ourselves more lost than Atlantis. And what do you do when you're lost? You ask a policeman...

The three uniformed cops are leaning against a street corner, chewing match-sticks. Three times I ask them how to get to Rhode

Island. Three times the cockiest one in the mirror shades replies "Whaaa?" Then his chubby mate adds: "Are you sure you don't mean Queens?"

The penny drops. With our cropped hair, combat jackets and "fag" English accents, the cops have mistaken us for biters of the pillow. I explain this to Mensi as I drag him away. "Fucking cuunts!" he explodes. "Let's do 'em, Gal."

"Tommy mate," I say. "They've got guns." He still fancies his chances – "They're WIMPS! Do I look like a fucking poof? We could smash them to fuck." But I manage to calm him down with the promise of beer. If I'd had me wits about me, I'd have blown them a kiss.

We have breakfast with Joe Strummer the next morning, who finds it all hilarious. We ask him why he's recently done a runner from the Clash. Strummer just shrugs and says: "I just thought, what the fuck..."

Joe and Iggy Pop both come down to the Upstarts show at the Peppermint Lounge. But the most incisive review comes from the punter who told Decca Wade: "Your singer's ugly and he can't sing. He just shouts and he doesn't do that too well." He could have been talking about the Gonads.

Cops were a frequent factor on Angelic Upstarts tours, but it wasn't always their fault. I was on the road with Jimmy Lydon's band the 4 Be 2s in Scotland once. Jimmy is John Lydon's younger brother. They were managed by 'rock entrepreneur' Jock McDonald (real name O'Donnell), a legendary music biz chancer. The band was supporting the Upstarts yet they were staying in the best hotels and tucking in to the finest steak and champagne every night. Jock even treated me to a fat Cuban cigar. How was this happening? Mensi was mystified. It turned out that Jock had just half-inched a load of WEA headed paper, forged the record company MD's signature and produced a letter guaranteeing that all of the 4 Be 2s' copious expenses would be met by the company – who they weren't even signed to. They got away with it for just about a week before Jock was led away in cuffs. If he'd been really smart, the prison governor would have then received a letter from the MD of EMI demanding his immediate release.

The 4 Be 2s were pretty much a Lydon family in-joke. John's other brother Martin appeared with them occasionally, as did John Stevens, better known on the Arsenal terraces as Rambo. McDonald was great company but a terrible influence. He took John to Dublin in 1980 where the ex-Pistol was banged up in Mountjoy Prison – known as 'The Joy' - for four days after getting roughed up by two off-duty garda in the Horse and Tram pub. They falsely accused John of assaulting them (he wrote PiL's 'Flowers Of Romance' album as a result and didn't go back to Eire until the Pistols played the Electric Picnic in Stradbally, 28 years later.) It was an outrage; the only thing Lydon ever did that merited choky was the more recent Country Life TV advertising campaign.

DREAD OVER DEUTSCHLAND
Judge Dread

December, 1980

"All right, get ready, here we go..."

JUDGE Dread tells me to meet him and his song-writing partner Ted Lemon in "our favourite restaurant" close to Hamburg's infamous Reeperbahn; a nice place to go window shopping, by all accounts. Prostitution is not only legal here – it's celebrated. Even so, I'm little startled when I arrive to find Dread and Ted at a table watching a black dwarf with an appendage as long and hard as a Polish surname servicing a large, willing and naked blonde. I hadn't anticipated that kind of starter.

"It's the cabaret," the good Judge chuckles. "Look at the size of that!" He indicates the dwarf's proudest possession. "It's got everything except an elbow."

"What are you having, Garry?" asks jovial Ted. Not the coq au van, I say. And the air is cleared. We laugh, we chat, we drink, we eat; Dread drifts off occasionally and pulls a few peculiar dreamy expressions...and then something even stranger happens: a cute female dwarf, a red-head in stockings and suspenders, emerges from under the table wiping her mouth. While we've been tucking in, the Judge has been enjoying an altogether different kind of nosh.

"If that was a crime, she's swallowed the evidence," the ruling king of rude reggae remarks with a grin.

Incredible... I've been on the road with Steve Jones and Paul Cook, the Damned, Max Splodge, Iron Maiden and Thin Lizzy, and yet it's taken an over-weight 34-year-old ex-bouncer from the sleepy Medway town of Snodland, Kent, to take my breath away.

It's like a scene out of a semi-comic porn flick, with dialogue to match. "My aperitif," he shrugs.

"She had a pair of teeth?" Ted banters.

"Nah, she took 'em out before she started."

Dread notices that I'm looking a little surprised. "Do you fancy one, Gal?" he enquires with a wink. "Just ask for a 'short'. I've left my American Express card at the door. Whatever you have, they just charge to the old account."

"American Express," chortles Ted. "That'll do nicely." Maybe later.

"Great puddings," says Dread, studying the menu.

"36Ds I reckon," replies Ted. This ain't rock'n'roll, and it's not genocide either. It's more like Confessions Of The Rudest Rude Boys In Town.

ALEXANDER Minto Hughes, known to his friends as Alex, his fans as Judge Dread and his enemies as "that dirty old bastard", is enjoying his second coming (ooh-erh missus, etc) here in Germany on the back of the 2-Tone explosion. The burly former nightclub doorman, bodyguard and debt-collector for Trojan Records became an underground legend in the early 1970s with his string of skinhead reggae singles: 'Big Six', 'Big Seven', 'Big Eight', 'Y Viva Suspenders'...all of them saucy, all of them banned by the BBC, and all of them chart hits. The dirty old bastard notched up two Top Tens, four Top 20s, and one Top 30. He then unzipped two more tasty 7inchers that pleasured the Naughty Forties. Sadly my personal favourite, 1978's 'Up With The Cock' ('Always asleep by ten o'clock, at six on the dot she's up with the cock' - about working on a farm of course), had fizzled out at a feeble 49.

"If it had been 69 we would have been happier," Dread laughs. His formula has remained unchanged since 1972's 'Big Six' (itself inspired by Prince Buster's far ruder 'Big Five', not to mention Verne & Son's 'Little Boy Blue'): simple effective reggae tunes married to nudge-nudge seaside innuendo ("That's an Italian suppository," wise-cracking Ted informs me.)

The madness starts as soon as I land at Bremen Airport. I'm strolling slowly through arrivals, more than slightly concerned by the number of stern-faced, submachine gun touting German plod about, when I'm knocked scatty by the kind of friendly pat on the back that would incapacitate a 25 stone grizzly bear. I spin round to clock the beaming face and comb-over barnet of Ted Lemon, Dread's portly, Pilsbury Doughman proportioned partner in rhyme. The Judge himself is decked out like a minor league football manager, wearing a flat-cap, shades, and a ticket tout's fur over-coat. He is in the company of a young and willowy fair-haired fraulein, the two of them obviously joined together by more than a common faith in the future prosperity of the European Economic Community. After a lingering embrace, Dread drags himself away and shakes my hand as if he's trying to wring Bollinger out of a house brick; and then, with a casual wave to the forlorn Teutonic temptress, we're off to Jah Lemon's waiting hire car.

"Well, that's me set up next time I'm in Breman, know what I mean Gal?" his legal highness guffaws, giving me a couple of gentle nudges in the rib department that would have put Big Daddy down for the count. "'Andsome or what? You wouldn't kick that out of bed for farting, would you, boy?"

We motor off towards Warstein and tonight's gig. In less time than it would take Mary Whitehouse to slag off a Carry On film, Dread is describing the many delights of Deutschland in the dirtiest of details. The great man is as happy as a dog with two dicks. It seems the world's second largest pop market has taken old Alex to its well upholstered bosom. He has enjoyed substantial second time around chart successes with 'Big Six' and 'Big Seven', not to mention his latest album, Reggae & Ska, and prime slots on a couple of TV promoted compilations. All of which has made Judge Dread more of a star here than either Terry Hall or Suggsy. And consequently, a sex symbol. You read that right. Dread is getting as much bed-time action as Mick Jagger on an all-oyster diet. My mind is not the only thing boggling.

"We're not gigging as such out here," he explains. "We're doing PAs on the disco circuit. I just jump up and sing over backing tracks. It's cheaper than coming out here with the band, and the punters are happy enough. Big old venues too, some of them are 4 and 5,000 capacities..." That may seem unlikely enough, but there's more... Dread has, it would appear, also become a cult star among the German aristocracy. Proper upper class Krauts: barons, nobles, counts – I think he said counts.

"These big-wigs are bunging Dread a grand a time to have him perform at their private birthday parties," reveals Cockney Ted. In Hamburg, at the Third World Club, one "little darling" coughs up £250 to reserve a stage-side table, and another £250 to persuade the Judge to do an extra encore. The extent of the ensuing after-sales service is best not referred to in detail in a respectable family publication.

But why? What can the German upper crust get out of watching a big English bloke with a beer gut singing about Winkle Trains and Doctor Kitsch with his injections? ('I push it in, she pulls it out/I push it back, she starts to shout/"Dr Kitsch, you are terrible/I can't stand the sight of your needle...")

"I can't really understand it," Dread admits. "Maybe because it's so down to earth and dirty they get turned on by it. Maybe it's a walk on the wild side for them. Or maybe it's like the way rich Yanks pay John Holmes" – a legendarily endowed porn star – "to turn up and screw their missus. Maybe now Dread's gyrating cock is fashionable.

"I don't really get the Germans at all," he goes on. "For a country that seems so permissive about what they let go on, they do strike me as being prudish. They don't like talking about it. I said to one promoter, 'Cor, I couldn't half do with a grind tonight' and he was really embarrassed."

We drive on, speeding south down the Fuhrer's autobahns towards Warstein, leaving behind countryside as flat as Olive Oyl's chest for picturesque villages, snow-kissed hills and woods. "Beautiful here innit," the Judge observes in a rare moment of pastoral reflection. "Lovely views. It's like driving through a Christmas card...Wouldn't it be good to get your cock sucked here? A wank in the Black Forest, that'd be something." William Wordsworth himself could not have put it better.

Our hotel is a tranquil watering hole set in the slopes of the lightly forested Haarstrang mountain slap bang next to a local nature reserve packed with bears, boars and other risky-looking critters. "I told the agency we liked wild night life," sighs Ted. "I might have known they'd get the wrong of the stick."

The place is warm and homely, attractively littered with the stuffed and possibly flea-ridden carcasses of deceased local mammals. "Taxidermy," observes Dread. "The only job you can give an animal a good stuffing and get away with it." It's a mounting problem...On the plus side the restaurant here serves the excellent local Warsteiner beer which is delivered to our table by a dishy blonde waitress who makes punk wild child Honey Bane seem flat-chested. The Judge is immediately smitten and wastes no time enquiring, "Kommen sie dahn das Papillion tonight, love? Frei! Gastliste!" A charming offer which the blushing busty beauty strangely declines.

"I think you offered her a free gasket," jokes Ted.

"She could blow my gasket any day," the spurned star replies. "She told me 'Nein', I think she guessed that's the length of my cock..."

THE Papillion Discotheque seems much friendlier. It's packed out with punters, and boasts a fine array of lagers which we partake of liberally in the interests of tourism, diplomacy and international good will. Dread has pre-recorded backing tracks with his excellent black and white British band back home. He divides his act into two half-hour sets, surprisingly mixing pop reggae arrangements of soft soul songs like The Tymes' 'Miss Grace' and 'Some Guys Have All The Luck' by the Persuaders, along with more familiar saucy standards such as 'Big Six', 'Big Seven' and a soupcon of Max Romeo's 'Wet Dream' thrust gamely into 'Rudy, A Message To You' – the Judge has been covering this 1967 Dandy Livingstone rocksteady original for years.

On stage, the big guy sports a fine pork pie hat and a double-breasted gangster suit; he performs like a randy Sid James at a Page 3 girl's wedding, ogling and leering, unzipping his fly, making vulgar gestures and frequent references to 'lieber-wursts' which roughly translates as love sausages. The audience loves every corny, horny minute. They're quick to dance, quicker to smile, and well up for singing along with the "uh-huhs", "right ons" und so weiter with a passion. There isn't a hint of trouble. "Refreshing," Ted Lemon points out, "when you consider how many of them umma louts they've got over here."

BUMBLING backstage a few beers after last orders, Ted and I are surprised (or maybe semi-surprised) to find the Judge engaged in, ahem, an intimate encounter with a busty, thirty-plus dyed blonde. The classy cracker smells like the perfume floor at Harrods and is weighed down with what looks like an entire shop window's worth of unsubtle jewellery. She offers Dread a lift home in her year old Mercedes. Lucky old Judge! Talk about have gavel, will travel...

We decide to follow behind. Before too long the classy seductress pulls off into a woody side turning and the imagination doesn't exactly develop muscles working out what's going on. The windows are misting up, and is that a naked foot pressing up against the glass? Mein Gott!

'Ikki takka, tikki taka, dikki taka, tai ya, whoop ai-ya, pussy catcha fire...'

Ted and I decide to hang about, just in case. I'm no longer entirely sure in case of what, but I had had a lot to drink. It's just as well we do, though, because the local cops waste little time turning up at the scene of the grind.

Herr Sergeant is a proper charmer with a military cop's crop and nostrils as piggy as his eyes, a real loss to the Gestapo. He gives us a good mouthful of guttural abuse and is none too happy with our "Nein sprechen German, Herman, me old fruit" replies. He gives us a look we could have shaved with and trots off to the passion wagon where thankfully m'learned Judge and his bit of Prussian posh are now fully attired. Later we get the full story: it seems Frau Howsyerfather is something of a local dignitary – we suspect a married one - and the Aged Wilhelm were just looking out for her. So no harm done, and just the one "Don't forget who won the war" hollered at their departing backs. But not loud enough for them to hear...

A beaming Dread jumps in with us. "What a brahma," he declares. "I would have banged her on the bonnet, but it was a bit tatters, know what I mean?" We head back to the hotel hoping for afters. Once again, the Judge gets more than he is expecting. The busty young waitress from tea time is shyly hanging around outside his room. Suffice to say the old Dread bedsprings were ringing out an Ode To Joy way into the small hours. Some guys have all the luck, indeed. All the 'Donald Ducks' as well... Not that Dread's good fortune prevents him from rising at the crack of dawn ("Lovely girl, works in the Co-Op" – Ted Lemon) and dragging us both down for breakfast.

"Got to make an early start," he cackles as he lays into a gut-busting post-coital feast. With my head throbbing, and rings under my eyes so big my nose looks like it's wearing a saddle, I wonder what the German is for Alka-Seltzer while silently cursing the smiling star and the next seven generations of his offspring. But as he and Ted start to reminisce it's hard to stay mad at him. Dread has stories so rude they make Ozzy Osbourne seem almost puritanical.

There was the time at the height of his fame in the UK when two women came backstage after his Brighton show and claimed to have "come three times" during the performance. They then produced vibrators as evidence and invited the whole band to help them come another three times before the club shut. On another occasion Dread got outrageously drunk with a friendly stripper who insisted on giving him head on a bench in Trafalgar Square – the details of which only came flooding back when he came round the next morning with his flies still undone and "little Dread standing to attention under a thin layer of frost." Then there were the usual array of chambermaids who preferred to make beds from the inside; and to top the lot the Judge tells of how a national household name DJ once pulled "a right old dog" on the road and was entertaining her in a ground floor hotel room. Dread moved in to watch through a gap in the curtains and promptly fell backwards like a pole-axed ox into the fish-pond...carpus interruptus.

Back in the car, en route to Stuttgart, Ted Lemon is giving a running, pilot-style commentary on the journey, thus: "Good morning ladies and gentlemen, this is your captain speaking; we're cruising at around 70 miles an hour at a height of six inches. The weather in Stuttgart is fucking horrible. Refreshments will be served shortly. Please return the air hostess to the upright position after use. Mesdames and monsieurs, je suis votre captain, nous sommes..."

Between giggles I ask who the pair rate as comedians. It comes as no surprise when they come back with Jimmy 'Kinell' Jones, the Cockney comic beloved by Iron Maiden and Status Quo, who inspired and heavily influenced TV's Kidbrooke-born comedy superstar Jim Davidson. Dread's rude repertoire has roots way back in popular culture. There are obvious similarities between the Judge at his best and the immortal Max Miller, who came up with rhymes such as 'When roses are red, they're ready for plucking/When a girl is sixteen she's ready for 'ere, 'ere...'

How far removed is that from the Judge singing: 'Little Miss Muffett sat on a tuffet/Knickers all tattered and torn/it wasn't the spider that sat down beside her/'twas Little Boy Blue with his horn'?

There are other obvious overlaps with seaside postcards, Carry On films and stag comics. Dread's humorous oeuvres trade in double meanings and dirty minds. And like his predecessors, he upsets the establishment. Judge Dread is the only person in pop history to have twelve (a dirty dozen) hit singles banned by the BBC. Yet most of his lyrics aren't explicit – there are no pricks or cunts, no fucks either. He's never effed and blinded like a Sex Pistol. "I think it's because we're the first people think we're the worst," Dread reflects. "Someone said to me the other day that the Ivor Biggun 'I'm A Winker' wanking song was as bad as my stuff, but we've never made a record that blatant. People associate me with Prince Buster's 'Big Five' but I've never released a song that crude either. I make humorous records. I don't release anything I'd be ashamed of. I couldn't do a song like Lloydie & The Lowbites did, 'Shitting On The Dock Of The Bay'." See, even the ruler of rude reggae has standards.

It still hurts him that his records were banned. "You hear far worse than what I do on the TV," he says. "When Benny Hill writes a saucy single like 'Ernie' they play it, but when we do just the same thing...it's like they put the knife in. It's not that I need the airplay, it's the principle. I've sold more than a million records all told, probably closer to two, so I'm entitled to go on Top Of The Pops and wave to the public, aren't I? Because the public is all I'm interested in. I'm not interested in the 'ego trip' of going on telly." He shakes his head. "They won't even let kids wearing my tee-shirts on the show," he says, adding "Prigs." Well it sounds like prigs...

Some critics, understandably perhaps, have called him a sexist, but you'd have to be a right prune to be seriously offended by his essentially puerile playground smut. Ted Lemon is less charitable.

"Oh yeah, they're the worst, the feminists, the ones who come up, look down their noses and say, 'I don't like you'. Two hours later they've got their drawers around their ankles begging for more. It's always the way."

A simplistic analysis perhaps, but you'd have to agree that the image of a knicker-less Germaine Greer, for example, begging for a length of judicial helmet is a funny one. I tease Dread by asking if rumours (which I've spread myself in the Sounds gossip column Jaws) about his good self and Bad Manners PR Sue Randy are true.

"Nah," he laughs. "She wanted to, but I didn't want to spoil her for other men. Oi! Oi! Look at that bleedin' snow, Gal. If we got stranded out here they'd have to send Alf Martin" (esteemed editor of Record Mirror) "out after us with a barrel of brandy around his neck."

"You're joking, that bugger would drink it all," retorts Lemon, no doubt libellously.

Alex Hughes became an over-night recording star at the age of 25, nine years ago. Before that he'd been a professional wrestler under the evocative moniker of The Masked Executioner. He'd also worked as a minder for the Rolling Stones. He was a male model for a day; he fed crocodiles at London zoo. He was a debt collector for Trojan Records until an axe in the head ended that chapter in his career. "I didn't even ask them to cut me in," he jokes.

Dread's music biz connections date back to the 1960s when he had worked as a 22 stone crop-headed doorman at the Ram Jam club in Brixton, where he first met Prince Buster, and the Flamingo in London's Wardour Street. He took the name Judge Dread from a Prince Buster song, but cites Laurel Aitken as an influence.

"Laurel made a record called 'The Rise And Fall Of Laurel Aitken' which was a rude one, y'know, rise and fall - we all know what that means, we know what was rising, it wasn't Tower Bridge. I think he's the only one who ever made me think there's money in all this."

Alex was running his own reggae disco in South London when he began toasting 'Big Six', written by him and Ted, in the clubs. When the song was first released on the Big Shot label in June 1972, it sold 68,000 copies to the ethnic black audience pretty much immediately. EMI picked up on the distribution and it sold a quarter of a million in just over a month. Even when they released

'Big Seven' months later, 'Big Six' wouldn't drop out of the charts. It stayed there for six months, selling in excess of 300,000 copies without a single airplay. The single became an institution, like the Richard Allen books. Every council estate tearaway had a copy.

A stream of similar filth followed, of which all except 'Big Eight' which was apparently left off "by mistake" are available on Dread's brand new 40 Big Ones compilation album. The Judge put more reggae in the UK charts than even Bob Marley. He began to fall from grace at the same time as the whole generation of glam rock stars, but like Slade and Gary Glitter, the big man was never forgotten and with the skinhead revival of the late 1970s so the Dread live audiences started to swell up (matron!) to a respectable size again.

"I'd been predicting the Ska boom for years," Dread says. "Remember it was 1975 when I wrote 'Bring Back The Skins'. The only things I frown on with the new lot are the sieg-heiling, which skinheads never did, and the violence, the way kids think they've got to go out and fight. I've always been involved with reggae music and I've never associated it with violence. Dread was the first white reggae hit obviously but now Bad Manners are carrying on that tradition. I think of Doug as sort of Baby Dread. I'm very pro that band. I like that type of thing. I like Madness too. But Selecter were too serious for me. Bad Manners are in it for a laugh and if you want to last as a band you've got to enjoy yourselves. The Specials are a different thing cos they were the first.

"I'll tell you what, I wouldn't half like to see the fat boy having a bunk up. I'd pay to see that. Imagine the state of him starkers, with that belly! He must have a little cock cos nothing grows in the shade. Of course, she'd have to go on top. And she'd still burn her arse on the light-bulb."

Dread goes on: "I love Britain obviously and I want to work back home again soon. Things like this tour are like a break for us. It's hard graft but it's relaxing. And everywhere is different. How many times can you go up and down the poxy M1? You get to know every bump on the road. I'm on nodding terms with the crows. Things like this keep you going because you don't know where you're going or what you're going to find when you get there. And obviously you've got to chase your ace. That's why I'm here. We're selling records here. Germany has become another Dreadland. Another couple of hits and we can bring the band over and do it properly and play the 10,000 seater venues. I want to play for the squaddies too if the NAAFI will book us."

Right now, Dread and Ted are working on a book and film project called Working Class Hero. Alex still sees himself as working class. "Dread was the first punk and I'll always be a punk," he insists. "I was saying bollocks and spitting and putting me fingers up when Johnny Rotten was still pissing his pants. I wasn't born I was hatched out by the sun. Someone had a wank on a window and I was there. The black people created a white reggae hero, a working class hero, and that's the way I will always be. I've never wanted a big house in the country. I've never wanted to lose my roots. And that's why it's great to see kids like Buster Bloodvessel making it. Working class kids, not stuck up idiots who think they're better than everyone else."

He laughs. "Stinky Turner, the 4-Skins, what a great name that is. If the 4-Skins, the Members and the Gonads got together with The Slits there is no telling what would happen..."

'Oh she is a big girl now, oh she is a big girl now/She got fat and we know how...'

Sadly, although perhaps not unexpectedly, our conversation soon deserts the path of decency, with the Judge offering me insights into his relationship with prostitutes. "I'd screw a brass, but I wouldn't muff it," he says thoughtfully. And Quadraphenia:

"That film got it all wrong, all that bunking that was going on at that party that never happened. And no fuckin' proper Mod ever followed the Who..."

The last time I see Judge Dread is at Hamburg airport. He comes along to wave me goodbye but gets distracted by a petite and heavy-breasted brunette, who he chases after offering such romantic endearments as "Come now sister, lay some sweetness on I-man, bloodclaat..."

Ted Lemon looks at me and winks. "If you can't beat 'em, join 'em," he chortles. "And if you can't join 'em, beat off..." Wise words indeed. And as tubby Ted wobbles off in hot pursuit a shocking thought occurs to me. I've been out here for the best part of a week and I've only mentioned the war once... I must be sickening for something.

CARRION SEX PISTOLS
Steve Jones

London, March 1979

"THE Sex Pistols never made cunts of the public," Steve Jones tells me. "It was the record companies we made cunts of." We're talking about The Great Rock 'n' Roll Swindle, the newly released double album, largely recorded after John Lydon had left the band. It's the soundtrack to McLaren's film which isn't due out any time soon. On one level it's funny; on another it's a real kick in the never-minded bollocks. If the intention is to present the whole chaotic Pistols explosion as one man's cleverly schemed money-making con trick then it's not only patently false, it's also insults the intelligence.

"The swindling thing ain't true," Steve. "That's just McLaren's little kick, making out he's conning everybody. It's his ego, y'know. I mean, he's saying he got us together but he didn't. He didn't do half the fucking things he says he did. F'rinstance, Rotten was Rotten when we first seen him, spiky hair and ripped-up t-shirts – nothing to do with McLaren.

"That's another thing, he didn't write the film single-'anded either, it was about four people. Tell you the truth I ain't got a clue how the film goes cos I ain't seen the finished version. I know there's lots of early film footage of us playing live..."

Okay, let's deal with the other controversies then; like Belsen Was A Gas. "Well, Sid wrote that," replies Jonesy. "He wrote all the words. Personally I don't give a fuck what any lyrics say. I just put a tune to 'em...Anyway, it's true. Millions of Jews were killed. What's wrong with telling people about it in a song?"

Don't you think the implication that the gassing was good – Belsen was a gas – is even a tad irresponsible?

"Yeah, I suppose so," the guitarist says, shifting uncomfortably. "But it's not meant to mean anything. It's just a snidey way of saying it was cuntsville the way they killed them people. Proper cuntsville."

In truth the tape of our beer-oiled conversation occasionally veers towards sounding like a Derek & Clive out-take, never more so than on the much pummelled topic of Friggin' In The Riggin' when I accuse Steve of fucking up the words to the historic rugby song, Twas On The Good Ship Venus. The figure-head was a nude in bed sucking a red-hot penis, I scold him pedantically. You sing mammoth penis! You even get the chorus wrong, where is the masturbatin' on the gratin'?

"Everyone keeps saying you must remember it from school," grins Steve. "But I didn't! First time I heard it was about a month ago cos I bought a book and copied the words out."

Tsk, and your school was approved and all! How did the protracted version of Johnny B. Goode come about?

"We were in Wessex Studio up in Highbury when we were doing Anarchy, we'd done about a hundred different takes and we just started fucking about. It's like when there are four of you in a police cell and at the start you're pretty straight and about five hours later you start going a bit nutty. That's what it was like for us when we'd been in that studio for a day and a half..."

Steve chuckles at the memory. He seems completely unchanged by all the fame and front page notoriety. And, incidentally, success hasn't fattened him up either. The 'Fatty Jones' jibes that NME slings at him couldn't be further from the truth, which is why I suspect he's keen to strike gym-themed topless poses for Chalkie Davies's pictures. This boy's not been pigging in the rigging. We're talking Fitty Jones here.

Steve is like any straight young working class geezer you might bump into in a London pub any day of the week. But then he is a young working class geezer...if not exactly on the straight and narrow. Stephen Phillip Jones is a former skinhead, a former football hooligan, a former thief...When I tell him I used to live on the White City Estate he reels off a list of names belonging to the kind of residents respectable people like you and I would have crossed the Westway to avoid.

Steve's boxer dad, Dan Jarvis, left the family Hammersmith home when he was two. He never got on with his stepdad. He played truant, dropped out of school and became a teenage kleptomaniac, falling head-long into a life of casual crime. After notching up 14 convictions he got 'popped' and did 18 months at a remand centre. He was a proper handful. Steve had been a skin –

he stole all the best clothes – and a regular on the terraces of all three west London clubs, although he freely admitted he never went to watch the football. "The fighting was what it was all about," he says. "I loved running rampage."

His best mate was Paul Cook, a carpenter's son. He'd been a good kid until he fell in with Jones at the Christopher Wren School in Shepherds Bush. From then on it was all downhill.

It was Paul's classmate Wally Nightingale who got the two of them into rock. He had a Les Paul copy, he had an amp – and the rest of the band's equipment was stolen wholesale and shamelessly by Steve.

Already an accomplished tealeaf and enthusiastic joy-rider, Jonesy lifted the best part of a set of drums from a BBC studio; and then bass guitars and amps were stolen from vans. Steve even targeted his hero Rod 'the mod' Stewart's mansion home in Windsor, nicking two guitars from the great man. But David Bowie's Hammersmith Odeon gig was the scene of his biggest heist. Steve and his cronies broke in the day before and half-inched the entire PA.

At first they called their band the Strand (taking the name from Roxy Music's Do the Strand). Wally played guitar, Paul, now an electrician's mate, drummed, Steve sang, and Steve Hayes was bassist. For a while a friend called Jimmy Mackin played rudimentary organ. But Steve's singing let the side down and Hayes and Mackin jacked it in.

It was then that they started hanging around at Malcolm McLaren's King Road boutique Let It Rock. Jonesy kept on and on at McLaren about what a great band they were. Eventually, Malcy shelled out for a rehearsal room so he could see them play. They were awful but there was something about them he liked. He introduced them to another local kid, his part-time shop assistant and ex-grammar-school boy Glen Matlock, who became their bass player and who Steve still calls unfairly "a middle class cunt".

Eventually, the band became the Swankers. Their set in 1974 consisted entirely of cover versions of 1960s standards: everything from credible Who and Small Faces to incredible old tat like the Foundation's Build Me Up Buttercup and Love Affair's A Day

Without Love. Kindly Uncle Malcolm's pocket money helped keep them afloat.

A trip to Manhattan for a fashion trade fare later in 1974 changed rock-music history. McLaren sought out the New York Dolls and persuaded the band to let him manage them. It was a disaster. Malcy decked them out in red-leather stage gear and had them perform in front of a hammer-and-sickle backdrop, an image guaranteed not to endear the noxious noise boys to 'Nam-burned Uncle Sam. Later, Johnny Thunders described him as "the greatest conman I've ever met".

You speak to New Yorkers and they'll tell you McLaren lifted most of the ideas of what became punk – the look, the style, the blank generation imagery – from the Big Apple's burgeoning underground scene, bands like Richard Hell & The Voidoids, Television and the Ramones.

When the Dolls finally dissolved, Malcy offered to manage Hell and Tom Verlaine. They knocked him back and he was on the first plane home, where he wasted little time reshaping the Swankers with his pirated images. Bubbling over with enthusiasm, he dedicated himself to recreating them New York rebel style.

Steve Jones was an average vocalist, but he turned out to be a gifted guitarist, allowing Malcolm to sack the eyesore Wally. Malcolm now needed a frontman. He tried many. He was blanked by Midge Ure. Out of desperation he even took singing lessons himself before finally chancing upon a lapsed Catholic speed freak from a Finsbury Park council estate called John Lydon who already looked the part.

Crane driver's son Lydon was a genuine eccentric. He wore a ripped and torn Pink Floyd T-shirt, which he'd customised with a felt-tip pen to read 'I HATE PINK FLOYD'. When he sauntered into SEX, dripping razor-sharp sarcasm, it was love at first slight. The kid was an original whose anti-style mirrored the look that McLaren had seen in New York. But John was no softie. The son of Irish immigrants Lydon was a working-class Arsenal fan. His older brother Jimmy and his best mate Rambo were proper street fighters; they had worn Clockwork Orange boiler suits to the matches. Later, when a mob of Notts Forest fans marched down the King's Road chanting "Kill the cockneys", John single-handedly charged at them screaming "Arsenal!" and, by his own admission, "frightened the living daylights out of them".

Plying him with Pils, Malcolm persuaded the pale but fearless youth with his wild angry eyes to audition over the SEX jukebox playing Alice Cooper's Eighteen ('I've got a baby's brain and an old man's heart . . .'). Johnny had everything: charisma, contempt, sulphate cheek . . . He also had green teeth, which were to win him a new nickname from Paul Cook's mum: Johnny Rotten.

At first Jones didn't rate him, but Malcolm was convinced he'd hit upon the right formula. He rechristened his dangerous brood the Sex Pistols. It was an uneasy alliance full of tension and mistrust, but it worked. McLaren masterminded strategy, Rotten sneered out angry contempt, Glen Matlock came up with the tunes, Paul Cook beat the drums and Steve Jones supplied the ferocious HM guitar wallop. There was nothing now to stop them. They had all the gear they needed: Cook and Jones, the self-confessed "working-class tossers", had swiped the lot. They had attitude, defined by their first songs such as Seventeen: 'I don't work, I just speed/That's all I need...'

All they had to do now was gig.

Almost inevitably, their first performance was a disaster. They opened for a Ted combo at St Martin's College of Art in November 1975 and proved about as popular as Oliver Reed at a feminist rally with his dick out. Students and Teds in the audience chucked bottles and hurled abuse until the student social secretary pulled the plugs. Undeterred, the Sex Pistols soldiered on. The next night they played the Central School of Art, where they actually managed to finish their savage 30-minute set. After that, they hit on the strategy of gate-crashing gigs, posing as the support band and terrorising audiences.

By January 1976, McLaren had all his selling points sussed out. "I'm gonna change the face of the music scene," he told Ray Stevenson, who was to become the Pistols' photographer. "All the music at the moment is by and for 30-year-old hippies. Boring. The Sex Pistols are fresh and young. They're kids playing music for the kids. Not some property tycoon singing My Generation. The Sex Pistols are from the streets and the dole queues. They represent most of the kids in this country." The rest you know...

So, how much dosh did you make out of the Pistols, Steven?

"Well I got a flat for £14grand and I've had £60 a week for about two years which has stopped now with Glitterbest going bust, and a couple of grand to spend. It ain't really much considering what we've done. Bollocks is still going up the charts but we've only seen one lot of royalties. Branson ain't paid us cos of this court case…" (To compress a very complicated legal ruck into a sentence, the court case was between Branson's Virgin Records and McLaren's management company Glitterbest; Malcolm lost it and the Pistols split).

But the Sex Pistols corpse is a gift that won't stop giving. Silly Thing, the third single from the Swindle album, is out this week. Not only would it go Top Ten, it also proved that all those "heavy metal" jibes at Cook & Jones are completely misguided. The boys can still knock out a blinding tune.

How do you feel about the band splitting? "Relieved," says Steve. "I think we went to America too soon and we was getting on top of each other what with Rotten being a real prima donna and having to keep an eye on Sid all the time. It was a real drag when he died cos I liked Sid, he was a great geezer; but he always said he wanted to die before he was 21. At least he was one of the geezers who meant it."

Steve didn't blame anyone for the bust-up though. "It really pisses me off when as soon as people do interviews they start slagging me off," he says with feeling, adding: "I don't hate Malcolm, I really like him; we've just both realised we don't wanna carry on working together. I don't hate Rotten either. It's just that whenever the Pistols were mentioned they had a picture of him so I suppose it's only natural that he started believing he was the Sex Pistols. The Public Image album is a load of toss. If Joe Bloggs had done it, it wouldn't even have got reviewed."

Steve has plenty of post-Pistols plans up his sleeves: more Greedy Bastards with Phil Lynott, a single with Joan Jett, maybe an album with her. "Paul wants to form a group cos he likes playing," he says. "And I have been thinking about it but then I get pissed off cos I think why the fuck should I want to play? We done it once!

"The best gigs were at the 100 Club," he goes on. "Every week you could see more kids coming. And you'd see one week they'd be there with long hair, the next week you'd see 'em with short hair and you really felt like you were doing something, starting something and it was great cos there had been nothing for ages. There was a reason for doing it, we was creating something. But if we was doing now I know I'd get pissed off after about ten gigs and pack it in cos it wouldn't be the same. I don't want to become a Boring Old Fart. I'd prefer to do song-writing and producing. That's what a lot of punk groups lack, good songs and good sounds which is what they need to keep the punk movement going.

"The only reason rock'n'roll lasted so long was because the songs were so good. That'd be a better way for me to contribute than touring round the fucking North for months on end."

Steve is still into "the wall of sound thing" and would love to produce the Skids. He pauses and volunteers some additional information. "Socially I've been shagging as usual, as many birds as I can," he says. "I don't think I'll settle down until I'm about forty cos, see, I've never met a bird I can have a decent conversation with.

"I ain't been ligging much this year but I still nick the occasional bit of stuff out of supermarkets just to see if I can still do it, just for a laugh really.

"When I think what I used to do...I'd be shit scared to do it now."

SHAM ENCHANTED EVENING
Sex Pistols Part Duh

Glasgow, four months later

Fast forward to July 1979, and I am up in Glasgow at the Apollo for 'Sham's Last Stand', along with 3,500 others. The strain of being seen as a yoof 'leader' to Britain's warring teenage tribes had worn Jimmy Pursey down. Tonight is supposed to be the band's last ever show. His exit on his own creation; his grand finale, his goodbye...

The stage at the Apollo is about twelve feet high and ten feet in front of it a thin line of bouncers restrain the front ranks of the crowd, kids who know they'll never see Sham again and who intend to wring every drop of enjoyment from what turns out to be a 100 minute show. 100 minutes comprising three different sets...and a short-lived false turn in punk rock history...

Set one was the past; all the old hits: I Don't Wanna, Rip Off (dedicated to Malcolm McLaren, as ever), Angels With Dirty Faces (for the Upstarts and the UK Subs), Everybody's Innocent, Ulster Boy, Borstal Breakout (with a kid risking broken limbs leaping on the stage from a side box), Hurry Up Harry...finishing with If The Kids Are United. Set two – the present – begins minutes later with Ricky Goldstein late of the Automatics replacing Doidie Cacker on drums for a taster of the new album and Jimmy explaining that tonight's gig is being recorded for a live album. The crowd go MacBonkers, but the bouncers are bastards and when the band strike up Borstal Breakout one more time it's like Grunwicks all over again down the front. Jeez.

Only one song could possibly round this part of the set off – the mighty new single, Hersham Boys with its rousing 'Robin Hood, Robin Hood, 'ere we go again' intro leading into a full-scale football-punk outing of outrageous Top Ten proportions. Hey ho, let's gooooo, and off the stage they troop to a touch of the old tumultuous applause till...SET THREE. Jimmy's idea of the future. Enter the Sham Pistols!

There are now five men on stage: Pursey, Dave Parsons, Kermit, Steve Jones and Paul Cook. Pursey steps forward to the mike and grins: "I once met these two geezers and I said, ain't you the geezers with that cunt McLaren who's killin' punks off...but they got rid of 'im and now, together WE ARE GONNA MAKE SURE PUNK COMES BACK ALIVE!"

The crowd roar out their approval, and Jonesy steps forward ringing out the unmistakeable opening notes of Pretty Vacant. It's a bit of an anti-climax because the guitar lead goes, but Pursey smiles and says "Just testing" and they belt through Vacant, a dynamite White Riot, an orgasmic If The Kids...

They sound so tight, so strong, so goddamn impressive that I am foolishly filled with optimism for what they could become.

BACKSTAGE, Sham veterans gather. The Sheffield Boys, the Benfleet Boys, Dean representing QPR and Ladbroke Grove, some lads from Tooting. All agree that tonight is one of the best, if not THE best Sham gig they've ever seen; but then we're all pissed and bigger things are obviously going down. Also backstage are Sham's manager Tony Gordon – never seen him at a gig before – and beaming Virgin supremo Richard Branson. Both are clearly sold on the lucrative possibilities of a permanent Sham/Pistols link-up. I speak to Branson. He is amicably non-committal, optimistic but as vague as a medium's insights. There are obvious legal hurdles to climb. Polydor still have an option on two Sham albums after the next one, one would be a live album, and Virgin are trying to talk them out of the second so that Cook, Jones and James Pursey can start recording as the Pistols immediately.

The lads themselves are heartily pissed off with the whole affair. Paul Cook moans about how shit things get when the lawyers take over ("They're the only ones what make any money") and Jimmy complains that they're being treated like "fucking bits of paper".

All seem enthusiastic about the future though. And high spirits reign on the long train journey home the next day, replete with Pursey attacking your intrepid correspondent with talcum powder – don't worry, I got the lanky bastard back with a blast of Brut; like garlic to a vampire it was. And there is a small table fire accompanied by a loutish sing-song of "Babylon's burning, Babylon's burning...." It is pandemonium! We knock back

Tennents, blare out tapes of new singles by the Purple Hearts and the Angelic Upstarts and fill the air with chants of "Charlie Harper!", "Freedom for Tooting!", "Freedom? There ain't no fuckin' freedom!" (from the soon-come Cockney Rejects debut ep), "Rude Boys!" and "Och, he only got his fingers up!" (believed to be a quote from one of the two young Scottish damsels smuggled into our hotel the previous night). Finger-licking good, indeed.

In a rare moment of sanity, Paul Cook complains about the interviews McLaren has been doing where he claims to have "planned" the Sex Pistols meteoric career – "a load of bollocks, he never planned nothing". I even take the opportunity to do some proper Robin Day style journalistic probing which swiftly establishes that 1) The proposed new punk super-group of Cook, Jones, Pursey and Kermit will be called the Sex Pistols. 2) They've already written "six or seven songs" including Jim claims one about Charlie Harper, called The Rag & Bone Man Who Saved Punk Rock. 3) The new Sex Pistols will be on the road by October.

Cooky confesses that last night's show was the first time he'd played live since the Greedy Bastards gigs with Phil Lynott. He also tells me (rashly, in retrospect) that "Jim is the only person who's come along who we can get on with. He's the same as us, see. We'd have started gigging again long ago if we'd found the right person, but now we're ready. Apart from the fact that he's a country bumpkin, Jim's all right. The great thing about Sham was that they appealed to the kids, and that's what we wanna do. The kids come along for a great time, they don't care what some wankers and trendies in the music press say."

Oh you silly things…

*Everyone was so pumped up with enthusiasm that nobody listened to Dave Parson who correctly observed "I don't think it's gonna last long because Jim always likes to be 100 per cent in control."

In the event Cook and Jones walked out of a recording session with control freak Jimmy the following month. Steve Jones said working with him was "worse than working with Rotten". Months later they launched the Professionals – they had one minor hit with 1-2-3 in October 1980.

Pursey's biggest mistake though was to announce a second farewell gig, this one in London at the Rainbow in Finsbury Park. I knew it would go tits up as soon as I left the tube station. The first thing I saw was BM bully-boy Matty Morgan smash a pint glass into a kid's face for his ticket.

There were only about forty of the knuckle-heads there but they turned the show into a disaster. By the time Sham came on stage, they'd built up a small army of some 200 skins around them and were running amok through the unseated venue.

Jim had hired in a bunch of Road Rats to do his security and they didn't want to know. The set last four numbers before the embittered ex-fans invaded the stage. The safety curtain dropped and Sham retreated.

The band did come back, eventually, but after seven numbers the Neanderthal Nazi tide surged on to the stage again. Pursey finally cracked. He demolished the drum kit, grabbed a microphone and shouted: "I fucking loved you! I fuckin' did everything for you! And all you wanna do is fight!" A tear rolled down his cheek. It was all over. Robbi Millar wrote in Sounds: "Jimmy said goodbye to London, and London kicked him in the teeth."

BLUE BEAT AND PORK PIES
Madness

November, 1979. Edinburgh.

'Madness, madness, they call it madness...'

SOD THIS for a game of soldiers. It's 8.45pm on a Monday evening, and it is officially thirty degrees below Eskimo Nell. It's cold, rudies; so cold that the local winos are drinking gin and anti-freeze; so cold that photographer Virginia Turbett's merkin is likely to migrate south for the Winter at any minute...so cold in fact that even happening band Madness are in danger of being downgraded from HOT to lukewarm.

Seriously, if you had a leak in the open air you'd have to snap it off. We're in serious danger of turning blue here, people. I may be stuffed on Stiff's freebie food and booze, but if they think for one micro-second I'm standing here looking like Papa soddin' Smurf...

Of course, any sensible soul would be at home with their feet up watching Porridge, and yet the doors of Edinburgh Tiffany's club are chock-a-block with chilly Billy-Bunters in their tartan scarves, thermal kilts and frosted sporrans. Like me, the kids ((c) Jimmy Pursey) are busting guts, toes, bladders and patience to get in out of the sub-arctic temperature and we are all getting nowhere fast. I look around in vain for a friendly St Bernard bearing brandy.

Scotland's capital city has, it would seem, been earmarked by some chinless government weasel as a testing ground in some fiendish mass freezing experiment, and quite frankly brass monkeys and mouldy taters don't come into it, pal. This frozen throng make TV's Adam Adamant in his block of ice look like John Bindon on the sun-kissed beaches of Mustique.

Ahead of Virginia and I, Stiff's token Scottish PR Andy Murray attempts to clear a path by handing out free Rachel Sweet singles to the Auld MacBill and almost gets nicked for his pains. Time for a few porky pies: "Scuse me mate I'm the bassist," Virginia claims illogically but loudly. It works! The crowd make like the Red Sea and Moses, leaving us free to swagger past the surly cops and straight through the doors, so we can thaw out and mark time at the jolly old bar until...it's show time!

This very first 2-Tone tour has lured more hardy explorers out into the life-threatening cold than the call of the North Poll. And quite rightly!

This is the greatest show on earth (for now at least), and young Scots Ska fans are here to bop until they drop to the non-stop, no-flop, mega-pop sounds of our current chart favourites...all for just £1.75 a head. What a MacBargain! Come on, folks, roll up, roll up, we're robbing ourselves here, and if we get six months you won't wanna be doing three of 'em. Going once, going twice, going, uh-uh, three times...

The Specials, Selecter and Madness are the name of tonight's game, the sound of 1979 (with just a sprinkling of noticeable exceptions). 2-Tone's souped-up Ska sparkle is merrily moonstomping its way up the charts and selling out the nation's polytechnics, Top Ranks and Tiffanys with this current, mammoth 'taking it to the people' tour.

But my brief for today's roaming in the gloaming exclusively concerns Madness and a feature of the Big One variety. Tuesday morning's BRMB chart shows their first Stiff single 'One Step Beyond' skyrocketing up 29 places for a brief respite on the back of those two little ducks, all the 2s, 22, before possibly catapulting them all the way into the Top Ten. Their debut single surprised everybody by going Top 20 from nowhere. Suddenly every A&R man in London descended on their gigs like thirsty tramps on a cider farm. Chrysalis and Virgin wanted them badly, but it was Stiff Records who got the band's inky 'x's on the contract – and then only because the label's big cheese Dave Robinson hired them to play at his wedding! (Dave later recalled: "They even got Elvis Costello to dance which was unheard of. They literary dragged him onto the floor...")

And now Madness are in the Top Thirty for the second time this year, the second time in ten weeks in fact. Not bad going for a self-confessed "bunch of absolute knobs". Yet four months ago few people outside of their mums had even heard of them...

Backtrack: I was stuck on a five hour train journey from Glasgow to London in the summer of '79 with no buffet and with only the company of those reprobate ex-Pistols Paul Cook and Steve Jones to keep me from crawling up a wall, and unless my memory deceives me Cookie spent a good half of the ride rabbiting on about this band called Madness who came from Camden Town and who were apparently a good laugh and well worth the effort of seeing.

As it happened a couple of days later I saw them advertised as playing the Moonlight Club in West Hampstead and thought I might as well check them out. It was a decision I've never regretted. It was just then that the hipper kids were waking up to the Specials, and obviously the whole Ska revival was new to most ears.

I'll admit that the first time I saw Madness they didn't impress me as much as either Dammers's dynamos or The Selecter had done. The Nutty Boys had some good numbers sure, but with their lyrics lost in the mix, they did seem, in retrospect, maybe just a couple of steps beyond a pub band. A good pub band, maybe, but a pub band all the same.

Similarly, the debut 2-Tone single 'The Prince' was decent enough but not as awesome as either its Special predecessor or Selecter successor, or indeed their own b-side cover of Prince Buster's golden oldie 'Madness', from which the band took their name. This was the song that hinted of the greatness to come. Fact is it wasn't till the release of their debut album at the end of last month that cynics were thoroughly convinced about the band. Their album One Step Beyond finally put the North London combo in a proper perspective, illustrating firmly their joint parentage – the glorious sixties Ska of the aforementioned Prince Buster and the joyous Cockney vignettes of Mr. Ian Robin Dury, whose abracadabra I'm particularly partial to.

The slower numbers in the set suddenly began to register. Like for example bassist Mark Bedford's 'Mummy's Boy' with its jokey, jerky foundation for excellent Lolita-reminiscent lines such as: 'Once went out with a London girl/Dirty weekend in a hotel/Broke it off when she got shirty/She was twelve/He was 30...' (Kind of Dury meets John Peel, that one). Even better was vocalist Suggsy and guitarist Chrissy Boy's 'In The Middle Of The Night' which in typical New Boots style sketches out the outlandish character of an underwear thief or knickers-nicker called George who 'in the middle of the night steals through your garden/Gives your hosiery a fright but doesn't say pardon...'

The wretched man's double life finally comes into the open however when newsagent Geo got the papers early and saw his own face.

Saxophonist Lee Thompson's borstal broaching tale 'Land of Hope & Glory' has a similar Dury-esque flavour, leading our office cynic to the conclusion that, "Ian Dury wouldn't record another New Boots and Panties so Stiff got someone who would."

The album is much more than that however, capturing the essence of teenage working-class London: a bluebeat base forged from too many Saturday nights beneath plastic palm trees mixed with breezy love songs and London low-life character sketches; the whole lot embellished by the band's perpetual striving after their own Nutty Sound (cue the usual 'sounds of summer fairgrounds' allusion).

Now you can properly appreciate their potential. They're altogether less intense, more, how else can you say it, nutty than their sometimes bleak Midlands colleagues. Madness are tapping in to a rich vein of Cockney culture and English humour. If they keep building on that, who knows how big they could be.

Madness haven't quite perfected the Nutty Sound yet musically, though they're breathing down its neck with the cheery Wurlitzer bounce of their budding 'Yakety Sax' Looney Tunes style instrumentals. And visually Chas Smash sums up the whole concept with his nifty nutty dance and multiple shouts of: "HEY YOU! DON'T WATCH THAT WATCH THIS!", "CHIPMUNKS ARE GO!", "ONE STEP BEYOND!", "THAT HEAVY, HEAVY MONSTER SOUND, THE NUTTIEST SOUND AROUND" et al.

Chas's close-cropped kid brother Brendan Smyth, a rascal/nuisance who's working on tour as product salesman and patience tester, is also a keen supplier of nutty phrases, such as "I've had a touch," (he's certainly touched), "Over and out," "Kamikaze!" and "On the case!" (If I were tour manager, I'd be on his case like a hotel porter chasing tips).

Brendan is joined on the band's travelling periphery by manager John 'Tin-Tin' Hasler, roadies Chalky and Toks (drummer Woody: "If Toks pushes you backwards, you know that Chalky will be kneeling behind you") and usually an away team of devoted fans including Totts and Whets, not to mention Lindsay, Wandsworth Harry (who apparently still owes Chalky £12 quid) and the fabled Prince Nutty. (At this point I'd like to mention my Uncle Bern too, because he's never had a name check in Sounds either).

THE band proper are Lee 'Kix' Thompson (saxes, some vocals, falling off chairs, walking socks, crew cut shades and 'burns); Chris 'Chrissy Boy' Foreman (guitar, Barry Sheene lookalike, family man); Mike 'Monsieur Barso' Barson (ivory-tickling, shades, infant moustache); Daniel 'Woody Woods' Woodgate (drums, vegetarian, Mo-Dette girlfriend); Mark 'Bedders' Bedford (bass, smiles, uh, bass); Chas Smash (shouts and t'ings), and Graham 'Suggsy' McPherson (vocals, vodkas, former butcher's boy).

The band hails from the Camden Town area of London, not that far a hike from the Cockney heartland of St Mary-le-Bow's in Cheapside. Their influences emerge quickly. One of their earliest musical activities was following Ian Dury's previous band Kilburn & The High Road in the wee years of this decade, Lee especially becoming great mates with the Grand Old Raspberry and is 'umper, Fred 'Spider' Rowe, and mightily bewitched by the Kilburns' saxophonist Davey Payne. The bluebeat bite came via Lee, Suggsy, Chrissy and Chas's private childhood record collections. For Suggsy and Chas, Ska and Trojan reggae were an important part of being skinheads which they were for years before the 1978 skin explosion ("When Sham come along I grew me hair," says Suggsy, cuttingly but not entirely truthfully).

Chas developed his unusual dance routine while pissing about to 'Liquidator' by the Harry J. Allstars (never complete to my mind without the "Skin'eads are back!" crowd chants as punctuation).

What we're really talking about is a group of teenagers, some mates, some mates of mates getting into music and eventually putting their own band together. Mike Barson could play the piano and he taught Chrissy the basic guitar chords. In 1976 they formed their first real band, the Invaders (AKA the North London Invaders) with Lee on sax, Chas attempting to play bass, manager John Hasler then on drums and various bods including Hasler trying out as vocalist.

Their musical approach was similar then, albeit far less successful, and they stabilised their line-up last year, changing the moniker at the Music Machine in Camden this January for the much more concise and definitive Madness. Progressing through pubs like the Dublin Castle and North London's gift to rhyming slang the Hope & Anchor, they were naturally intrigued by early media reports about the Specials. Extended feelers on both sides resulted in valuable support dates and contacts at a time when music paper hacks were starting to get wind of the whole new scene.

Reviews followed, chased hard by a feature in Sounds in July, their debut one-off single on 2-Tone in August, Stiff signing in September (just three weeks after playing at Dave Robinson's wedding reception), the release of their debut album in October and the start of this titanic tour. That's one hell of a ride.

SEPTEMBER, October, No wonder I'm here, battling with barbarian barmaids who have never heard of light & lagers and hiding my pad and pen so I can forget about taking notes and just soak up the show. And no I'm not going to get into the whole who-outplayed-whom argument at this stage; suffice to say none of these bands are third class tickets, and Madness in particular have tightened up (reggae pun, be still my aching sides) almost beyond belief. The nutty lads are currently a more than fair investment for your hard-earned LSD.

Their set, for those who like to know these things, is: 'Tarzan's Nuts', 'Mistakes', 'Believe Me', the sublime 'My Girl', 'Swan Lake/Razorblade Alley', 'Land Of Hope & Glory', 'In The Middle Of The Night', 'Bed & Breakfast Man', 'One Step Beyond', 'Rockin' In A-flat', 'Nightboat To Cairo', 'Madness'. Encore: 'The Prince' ("Guess who this one's dedicated to...")

Live, the band are a real visual treat – as lively as you like, funny and easy to love. During the tightened-up Tchaikovsky reworking of Swan Lake, Suggs and Chas (the self-styled Coco Brothers) bump bonces – real nut crackers, see - and go through some pretend aggro moves completely in time with the beat. On 'Night Boat To Cairo' (which comes with fog horns and sax as raspy as a smoker's cough) the two twerps remove their pork-pie titfers and put on fezzes. By Tommy and Cooper! They're natural clowns, these boys; the point where Ska meets slapstick and whacks it in the mooey with a big fat custard pie.

Chas Smash wasn't even in Madness to begin with. He was a fan who, according to Danny Baker, "raised stage invasion into a fine art" and in the process became 2-Tone's first authentic star. Watching Madness for the first time, Chas (real name Cathal Smyth, Carl to his friends) was always the one you remembered the most. Most of tonight's audience are seeing all these bands for the first time live, and the beams on their faces say it all. This was worth risking hypothermia for. The most moving moment of the entire night however is the final encore, after the Specials' own sparkling performance, which featured all three bands and several fans dancing through that old Symarip classic, 'Skinhead Moonstomp'. (Chrissy Boy tried to entice me up for vocals but, sad to say, I lost me Aristotle, thus preserving the ear-drums of many an unsuspecting Edinburger.)

Puritanical viragos will be pleased to learn that there was a notable absence of both booze and carnal conquests back at the hotel after the show. No Glasgow kisses either. Most people just hit the hay. Given the number of excited women-folk at the gig, that really was madness. Brekkers the next morning is a hectic, not to mention chaotic affair, what with Selecter Desmond Brown hollering for bloodclaat bacon sarnies and Neville from the Specials dishing out random insults a la "Rasclaat", along with hangover-aggravating shouts of "MONKEYMAN!" My, the staff look pleased. Before too long, the carnage spill over to the hotel foyer which rapidly turns in to Casey's Court as well, with poor old Andy Murray flying around like a blue-arsed fly, tugging lumps out of his barnet, trying to organise his troops for photos with Virginia Turbulent and then, ta ra, the serious interview...

'FUCK ART LET'S DANCE' is the Madness slogan. The band themselves don't put much store on the old jaw-jaw either and are keen to leave out any highfalutin' sociological ramifications both to what they do, and what 2-Tone is. However, unfortunately, any Madness feature would be incomplete without some discussion of their sometimes heavy skinhead following, including a solid lump of neo-Nazi British Movement numbskulls who recently went completely out of order bottling Orchestral Manoeuvres In The Dark off stage at the Electric Ballroom. In return Madness fans got indiscriminately attacked by a misguided and heavily tooled up Red Action mob at Hatfield Poly earlier on this tour...

The band's sincere anti-racist stance has not subsequently been helped by an article in the NME which dumbly misinterprets Chas Smash's comments about neo-Nazis in their audience to make it look as if Madness has no problem playing to extremist rightwing thugs...

"Now personally I hate all this BM business," says Labour voter Suggsy. "But a lot of the kids get taken in by it. When I was 13 all the kids used to go down Brick Lane in the East End, where that lot sold their papers, and it's easy to get pulled along by all of that; which is precisely why I don't turn round and say 'Kill 'em all.' They're just ordinary kids being like their mates, and the BM thing gives them a sense of identity. That's all. It doesn't mean a lot to most of them outside of that. The way I see it, if they're all dancing to black music that means more than shouting at 'em or slicing 'em up. Personally I'm more worried about violence at our gigs..."

Chas agrees, adding "If they fuck around at our gigs we don't wanna know. They're out."

Suggsy goes on: "These kids fight all the time; it's what they do for fun. So we say just don't do it at the gigs...obviously it'd be far better if they didn't do it at all..."

Chas recalls three lads who the band had banned because of the trouble that they had caused trouble at Madness gigs. He says: "The other day the three of them came up and asked if it was all right if they came back and promised to behave. Because they do care, y'know. Underneath the front, they care."

"Yeah," agrees Suggsy. "Don't forget that at the Dingwalls gig, it was the skins who went around stopping all the trouble."

"One thing you can never do is generalise about skinheads," says Woody sagely. "And when the audience get dancing there's nothing else on their minds except enjoying themselves. But we get all kinds at our gigs, not just skins."

Suggsy sums up the band's aims succinctly. "Entertainment," he says firmly. "The nearest thing you can say is that all we want to do is have a good time, get better at what we're doing, people enjoy it, make some money and be successful. We're not trying to read anything deep into it."

SO what next? Surely they'd have more Mad plans than a Bond villain? Well, they leave the 2-Tone tour after the next two Scottish gigs (they'll be replaced by Dexy's Midnight Runners). Then there are three London home crowd shows at the Electric Ballroom followed by their first foray into the USA – a nine day One Step Beyond Tour of small clubs and kharzies. ("We wanted to get there before the Specials, and we did," Suggsy told the music press later). Then it's back to rehearse new numbers – they've got four in the pipeline, before they head off on a headlining UK tour of their own. More dates, in Europe and hopefully the USA, will follow before they go into studios in March, with a view hopefully to releasing their second album in April. Busy boys, eh?

They have some nice things about Stiff Records, and they ask me to convey another cryptic message to a certain 'Mr Bentley' ("We warned him but we still beat him to it – though he's probably still in with a bit of a chance... he'd better watch Spider though, he reckons he's gonna come with us. Says it's more of a laugh.") And then the lovable lunatics are spirited away on the coach for Ruffles in Aberdeen.

Watching them nutty train their way through the hotel's revolving doors, I sank back on a bar stool and decided the perfect metaphor for Madness would be a couple of comprehensive kids bunking off school one May day, dodging the train fare down to Margate, and spending the whole day pissing about in the famous Dreamland funfair, pulling birds, pigging down chips and getting legless on cheap lager...That probably just about sums the nutty spirit up.

ALL MOD CONS
The Jam

May, 1979. Sheffield

"It's just Pop music and that's why I like it. It's all about hooks and guitar riffs. That's what the New Wave is all about..." – Paul Weller

IT'S the first night of The Jam's latest UK tour, and we're relaxing before the show in the hotel bar: me, Weller, thirsty Bruce Foxton, nice-guy Rick Buckler and a few others. Out of habit I ask for the set-list, even though I know all their songs backwards, and Paul takes the trouble to write it out for me in my notebook.

I read it back approvingly. Let's see, there's 'Modern World', 'Strange Town', 'Place I Love', 'London Girl', 'Angels With Dirty Faces', 'Complete Control'....do what?

"Just testing," the allegedly 'intense/moody' Weller laughs, adding a curt "We know you're gonna review it from the bar anyway. All you journalists are the bleedin' same."

Bloody cheek. I'm thinking about calling my brief but after the show, Foxton ups the ante. "We knew you were at the gig," he says. "Because we saw your chin hanging down over the balcony like a net curtain..."

Now this is not the first reference to my alleged "double chin" that I'll endure this trip from the little rat-faced bastard, nor sadly the last. Muppet-brained Foxton spent most of the coach ride and pre-gig imbibing time muttering such pleasantries as "Fat chops!", and "Whatever you do don't mention the chin."

Bruce reckons I have more chins than a Hong Kong phone directory, and that my favourite tipple is double chin and tonic.

Some might suggest that this disgraceful tirade indicates a deep degree of self-loathing on Foxton's part. Some might retaliate with low references to his own looks, along the lines of 'the face that launched a thousand horror movies'. Not me. I'll merely let slip that the Sheffield University security men didn't have a clue who the fox Bruce was and refused to let him back-stage from the bar before the show, leaving him hanging about panicking like a slightly pissed plum...Karma, baby.

THE Jam are good tonight. They're hot, in fact. So hot you can see the sweat dripping from Paul's fingers as he smashes and slashes at his Rickenbacker. They've got it all, this band: passion, a look and a unique sound. The Jam deal in terrific high energy songs with hooks and intelligence; his tunes and his words are worth hearing...

Off-stage, Paul Weller lives and breathes music. He sees what the band do as "pop music – that's all new wave is, Today's Pop Music for Today's Kids."

Meeting the coach at Staples Corner, I sit at the back with the sharp-dressed son of Surrey and his girlfriend Jill. I'm surprised to find that he doesn't share my glee at this morning news of that nice Mrs. Thatcher's election (Note to readers: kids, this is satire).

"How could a working class person vote Conservative?" he asks with genuine astonishment. Eh? Didn't Weller tell the NME he was voting Tory? Well, yeah, but that was "a private joke to wind up the Clash," he says.

"Thatcher made me laugh when she said she was a self-made woman," he fumes. "Of course she was - she had mummy and daddy's self-made money behind her." (In fairness, Maggie's Dad Alf Roberts was a greengrocer, not exactly a Rothschild).

"Try telling the girl behind the counter at Woolworth's she can be prime minister. 'Sorry dear, no qualifications. Can I interest you in a new car or an electric toaster?'"

It crosses my mind that the girl behind the counter at Woolies could always go to night school and get some qualifications if she were that bothered, and what the hell is wrong with toasters anyway? But Paul has already moved on to the subject of self-styled rock 'n' roll messiahs – he remains as distrustful of musicians with more good causes than good songs as he is of the notion that giving someone a guitar automatically gives them insight into current affairs and world politics...

The son of builder John and Ann, a cleaner, he was born in Sheerwater, near Woking in Surrey and grew up in a small terraced house with an outside bog and no heating. He was christened John William Weller, acquiring the Paul along the way as a tribute to McCartney. At school (Sheerwater County Secondary) he was a Beatles obsessive. But being out in the sticks, he never went to concerts. The first time he ever stepped foot in the Marquee was when the Jam played there.

He played in a lot of working men's clubs and pubs though, often between the bingo, watching blokes go round selling whelks and cockles. He started playing at 13 in a duo with school pal Stevie Brookes. Rick Buckler made them a trio, Foxton joined last.

They were a four-piece till Brookes left in late 1974.

His parents were very supportive, John an ex-welterweight boxer ran them everywhere, and they turned up as a family with his younger sister Nicky for social club gigs. Now John manages the band; Ann runs the fan club.

Paul left school at 16. He was never academic, hating the "crap" books he had to read for English lessons. He tells me he got all the education he needed from the lyrics of Lennon and McCartney, Ray Davies and Pete Townshend.

He's never seen the Who and doesn't like anything they've done for years. But boy his eyes light up when the subject gets round to Motown, Stax, Otis Redding, Wilson Pickett, the Monkees, and sixties beat group, the Creation. There's a lot of solid Mod in Paul's record collection.

What's it like to be the daddy of a movement? I ask.

"Don't blame me," he laughs, but you can tell he's chuffed, openly enthusing about the Chords, the one Mod band he's seen so far. He shows a lot of interest in what's happening at the grass roots and pumps me for info. "The spirit seems good at the moment," he says. "But I don't think the unity will last. Same as punk, once the record companies get involved and they're all competing then no-one will speak to one another. The general consensus is that it will be dead by August. I'll still be wearing me mohair suit in ten years time."

Paul Weller spends most of his money now on clothes, records and booze – just like he's always done.

THE New Mods' admiration for The Jam continues unabated, which is why about thirty faces from the East End (and Lou from the Elephant) have trekked up here to Yorkshire, where the M1 is cobbled, to see them play tonight. The plan is to pull local girls or sleep rough in cars, but many of them end up sneaking past the night porter into our hotel, and blagging empty rooms.

It's quite fitting that this new movement has coincided with the Jam's rise from the doldrums of last summer to new artistic peaks. All Mod Cons, the Jam's latest album, came out in November. I thought it was remarkable then and it's continued to grow in my affections ever since. In retrospect it was the album of 1978, no contest. 'Strange Town'/'Butterfly Collector' – the double-barrelled last single – hit the same creative high and was the band's biggest seller since 'In The City'.

"'Butterfly Collector' was about an actual person," Weller confides (actually, a groupie; suggestions on a postcard please).

"Whereas 'Strange Town' is more of a flow of ideas, it's a free form poem, and it combines a lot of ideas. Like there's the UFO theme, and there are lines like 'You're betrayed by your accent and manners'. I used to think class war was a myth but you find whatever you do, the way you talk and the way you are marks you out."

It's going to be difficult to follow 'All Mod Cons', I suggest.

"Yeah, which is why we're not going to try," he parries. "We hope to get an album out by the Winter. I think it'll be a lot simpler than All Mod Cons and that's all I can say. I've got a few ideas for songs but we haven't had a chance to write on the road."

And The Jam have been on the road for longer than tarmac, following November's mega UK tour with Germany and France in February and March, and the States and Canada last month.

"America was great," Paul enthuses. "Especially LA where we got really excited and the audience smashed up the seats and threw them on stage. It was a real electric feel and the kids were great. People were coming five or six hundred miles to see us. Great!"

They had just eight days off before they were off on sixteen British dates. They haven't even had time to rehearse for tonight...

Battling through the complexities of Sheffield Uni and local accents ("Eee, trouble at t'gig") we eventually locate the venue. Hammersmith Odeon it ain't.

"Jesus, the stage is bigger than the hall," Paul notes. Bruce channels the spirit of Python to declare: "Eee, it's like a shoebox in t'middle of t'road." Still, it holds 1500 people, we're assured, so, sound checks done we head to the hotel to watch Mork from Ork cavort and sink a few Forsyte Sagas. The early evening rapidly degenerates. Bruce throws ham rolls at me, I throw ham rolls back. Rick throws ham rolls at my snapper side-kick Virginia Turbett. (Odd, bands normally offer her sausage). Then Bruce brings up the chin again, and I challenge him to come clean about his dubious sex life.

"Pass me another bum, this one's got a crack in it," announces Paul, in keeping with his entirely serious sage-like image, which puts an end to it all.

Weller is actually so nervous about the show he throws up. (Although that might just have been the effect of looking at Bruce for too long...)

Paul's dad John is a revelation. He's a proper Londoner, a portly fella with a mess of silver hair and a voice like Mike Reid – the Cockney comic not the DJ. Nice bloke too.

WE head back to the gig in good spirit. I hang out with the London boys while the band get changed and listen to Paul's personally compiled warm-up tape of classics: 'Long Shot Kick De Bucket', 'Reggae In My Jeggae'...heaven. This kills a bit of time before the three of them catapult on stage and Weller hollers: "This is the modern world!" – pronounced "wowld". And we're off.

I'm up in t'balcony overlooking the front of the audience who go seriously barmy from the first power chord. And I'm torn between the triangle on stage and the crazy crushed crowd below me, a hot and squelching human sea pushed and shoved wildly to the left and right.

Inevitably the stage wins out. Paul stands be-suited legs apart, slightly stooped over his creamy Rickenbacker. He looks like an angry stork. Bruce slugs away on his black bass, his face getting redder like he's about to spontaneously combust; while Rick's dead centre in a shirt and tie beating away seemingly oblivious to the heat: the three forces merging in a mighty geometric explosion of perfect punk/pop/modern r'n'r...call them what you will, I think they're sensational, the next great roll of the rock anthem dice. Intelligent. Musical. Looking backwards and forward at the same time, like Janus. This ain't Pop, it's Super Pop. And from where I'm standing there's not an ounce of Kryptonite in sight.

FOR fifteen blistering numbers the crowd dance, pogo, crush each other, faint and punch fists and fingers at the stage. Some of the London Mods stumble out exhausted muttering "not as tight as Paris" and "the audience is wrong" but no-one else is complaining.
  'Mr Clean' is an early high, powerful and accusatory, losing none of its intensity on stage. When Paul sings the chorus, the audience nearly drown him out: 'Cos I hate you and I hate your wife/And if I get a chance I'LL FUCK UP YOUR LIFE, Mr Clean!' Is that seen?
  'Butterfly Collector' is a brave live choice, handled exquisitely, with Weller standing alone in the spotlight for the verses with the audience slowly clapping in time. Then there's 'Away From The Numbers', 'Strange Town', 'A-Bomb', 'Tube Station' – fistfuls of modern classics.
  The NME's Ian Penman recently accused The Jam of "writing singles for a mythical juke-box" – as if the very act of penning songs people might enjoy is a crime against artistic integrity. Well, I've got news for you, pal: there's nothing mythical about the juke-boxes you'll find the Jam on these days.
  The distant echo of far-away voices playing far-away games...Penman and his ilk wind me up like the proverbial clockwork orange. Who would have thought that rock 'n' roll, a music forged for fun and against privilege would have spawned the self-indulgent, insular mind games that occupy today's music writers and 'genuine new wave musicians' – the cold and uninvitingly pompous twats with all the answers in formulas we're not smart enough to understand.
  Smug, self-satisfied condescending snobs look down on you, your tastes, the bands you like, the records you buy... They think they're better than you, but they never soil their hands, never make a stand on anything tangible. They never do anything worth doing in their entire miserable existence.
  Yet despite them, laughing at them, the late seventies revel in glorious popular music, and carving their name in big bold letters at the very top of the tree are the Jam, with battered penknives,

Johnson and Johnson blazers and a dazzling array of musical wares.

The Jam: marrying refreshing rock insights and bitter-sweet sensitivity. The Jam: music for the modern world from a band who've learned to live by hate and pain.

The Jam are NOW! And of course no-one lets them get away without encores. 'Heatwave', 'Standards', 'Bricks & Mortar', 'The Batman Theme', 'David Watts' with the audience bellowing "be loik" and mouthing "Watts" but thinking Weller, Buckler, Foxton. Well maybe not Foxton. Then the lights go up and they snake out slowly into the cold night until everyone's gone, even the band, except for me, sitting in the bar with my set-list, patiently waiting for 'Angels With Dirty Faces' and 'Complete Control'...

Postscript: Mr Paul Weller is 21 on May 25. I caught up with Paul's sister Nicky Weller last year and interviewed her about The Jam exhibition at the ICA. Nicky reminded me that once Polydor had signed the band her father John, a regular Del-Boy, used to blag his way into the record company building every day, find an empty office, and use their facilities to do band business. He got away with it for about a year!

Historical footnote: the first time I saw The Jam was on April 17th, 1977, at the Roundhouse, opening for the Stranglers. A month later I caught them again at the Rainbow in Finsbury Park, supporting The Clash (9th May), with the Buzzcocks, Subway Sect and the Prefects. This was exactly how my review of their gig that night appeared in my fanzine, Napalm:

Everyone is standing for the Clash. Down the front they haven't got a choice – they've ripped up all the seats! It's been one of those nights.

The Jam get better every time I see them. They grab the crowd from the minute they come on stage. They're as tight as a Vulcan death grip, and they're sharp and different too. They've got songs, hooks, energy and Paul Weller is playing a Rickenbacker as smart and red as any Joe Strummer lyric. Their best tunes are the single 'In The City', 'Away From The Numbers' and 'Art School', two of which are mini-anthems. Weller wants to say, he wants to tell us, about "the young idea..." he doesn't say what it is but I'm happy to settle for what the Jam do deliver: energy, harmonies and suits. My only moan is they also trample old soul songs to death, but give em time. Their set is young and so are they. May, 1977

RUDIES UBER DALLAS
The Selecter

Texas, May 1980

IT TAKES a while to sink in that it's all for real: the sheer, breath-taking size of the place, the drawls and y'alls, the ten gallon titfers, Baptist fire and brimstone on breakfast TV, battalions of bronzed blondes who just lurv letting it go to their heads, and that big yellow sun that looks like it's just come unstuck from a packet of Cornflakes. Yup, it's pow'ful hot in Texas, boy. Pow'ful confusing too...

It was my idea to drag the Selecter along to Southfork Ranch in Plano, so that we could all pose ironically of course under the famous sign familiar to all viewers of TV's Dallas, and maybe snatch a glimpse of knee-high nympho Lucy Ewing (the soap's poison dwarf) in her bikini. Or at least catch Miss Ellie hanging out her smalls. Except now we're here, Desmond Brown doesn't look too impressed. "Where's all the oil wells, mister?" the organ-grinder moans. "I thought this was Texas!"

Bob Marley lookalike Charley Anderson swings his skinny, dipstick frame up on to the ranch fence, looking like an over-sized stick insect in Compton Amanor's huge, bug-eyed shades. "One day boy, all this will be yours" he drawls, his shock of red dread-locks shaking in merriment.

Move over Larry Hagman, there's a new boss in town. JR is now officially Jah Rasta, for just a dog-gone minute at least.

Arthur 'Gappa' Henderson laughs and grabs a handful of bush which he sucks on like a yokel's straw in a perfect country bumpkin impression. "Yippie", "yee-haw" and "howdy y'all" we yelp and holler to unimpressed passers-by. Dang, this is fun. "We ought to do a Ska version of the Dallas theme for our next single," grins Neol Davies. With 'Rawhide' on the b-side, I suggest.

But then we notice that the Selecter's paunchy tour driver Romain Reynolds isn't laughing.

"In this state, the people who own the ranch have the right to shoot you dead for trespassing like y'all just did," he grumbles. And just in case we think he's laying it on thick, Romain points

71

out the bullet holes in the side windows of the bus where furious locals had let fly at the last band he'd been transporting around the Deep South. You don't get that with Dolly Parton, who Romain normally drives for, a fact he mentions just once or 97 times.

If that's not enough to dampen our spirits a flat-bed truck motors in from Hogge Road carrying four burly geezers who look, aptly enough, about as happy as a herd of prime pigs in a pork pie factory. The temperature is high, somewhere in the 90s, yet the looks they're giving us are nippier than topless night in an Eskimo bar. One of them is clearly caressing a baseball bat. He doesn't appear to have a ball.

Romain wanders over and a heated conversation ensued. He comes back grim-faced and tells us to get on the bus and keep quiet. It's only later that we find out how frequently the word 'nigger' had figured in their exchange. Don't you love it when a Klan comes together?

THERE'S racialism the world over of course, but in our limited experience of Texas the bigotry seems different here. In-bred, institutionalised. The norm. "Appalling," Selecter singer Pauline Black observes simply. So where will that leave a bunch of mixed-race Brit blue-beaters with a message of 2-Tone tolerance and implied socialism? Strung up in front of burning crosses was one particularly vivid vision in my jet-lagged mind. Another involved multiple Mafia bullet shots from a grassy knoll.

"It's different for the Selecter," Romain explains. "Because they're a band and because they're British. But there are still a lot of places I wouldn't take them." Without changing his expression at all, he adds, "Why, only last month in my home town they shot a black man dead for being down town after dark." So a little bit more of a challenge than playing Manhattan or LA, then...

It's true to say that Pauline nearly died on this tour. But that wasn't down to any good ole boys and their Louisville Sluggers. It was more a case of her not reading the instructions on the water bed in her motel room. "I was pretty exhausted after our second US show in Portland, Oregon," the Queen of Ska recalls. "And I just collapsed onto my bed as soon as we got back from the gig. A couple of hours later, I woke up feeling like hypothermia had set in! You're not supposed to use the bed without heating it up first. They had a little typed notice telling you this but I hadn't seen it. I dread to think what would have happened if I hadn't woke me up. They'd have probably found my corpse in a block of ice. Seriously, it took two hours for my teeth to stop chattering."

Charley suffered for his art too. When the Selecter played Los Angeles, they stayed at the famous Tropicana on Santa Monica Boulevard, where the bassist managed to put his back out in the shower while entertaining a couple of fans, who just happened to be female, and gorgeous, and naked. Talk about Too Much Pressure.

Charley was in so much pain the band had to scrap two shows. The bill that followed the subsequent visit from Jack Nicholson's chiropractor is believed to have hurt even more. Naturally at the time, the press were fed the bullshit PR line that he'd pulled a muscle leaping about on stage.

The Selecter hit Canada first in mid-April, and have been doggedly slogging their way around the USA ever since to the same kind of small but solidly fervent adulation that had greeted earlier 2-Tonic forays by the Specials and Madness, selling out respectable 1,000-capacity venues to the hip tip of the vast US audience iceberg.

Last October's 'On My Radio' single has been selling steadily on import, Stateside. Too Much Pressure, their debut album was released here at the beginning of March, impacting on all three of the major US charts. It was still rising slowly as I caught up with them. The influential trade mag Billboard had made the album its hit pick one week, while the LA Times ran a glowing front page review of the band. The UK Sun has been over. Even those hippy horrors at Rolling Stone are covering them.

A-List stars are turning out for them too. Bubbly Bette Midler burst in back-stage at LA raving about the band – David Bowie had apparently slipped her a seven-inch (writes Benny Hill) in New York last December.

Singer Marsha Hunt came by the Tropicana to interview the band – Pauline reveals that Desmond's opening line to her was "I've always wanted to fuck you." The smooth-talking bastard!

(Well he is the organist...). While strolling bone Mick Jagger and Jerry Hall turned up at their Hurrah's show. And danced too...

Not a bad draw for Coventry's most motley crew.

Alas, there was no stellar turn-out at the Dallas Bijou club. No JR, Bobby, or lip-quivering Sue Ellen. Neol Davis, the main brain behind the whole Selecter enterprise, and a man described by Ms Black as "Fonzie without the muscles" fills us in on the evening's schedules. It seems that Pauline & co will be performing between the resident heavy metal band and a Wet T-Shirt competition. Photographer Ross Halfin's face lights up. Ms Black noticeably winces.

We arrive to find an audience of caricature cowpokes straight from central casting. The geezers sport a veritable sea of ten gallon hats, checked or embroidered shirts, denim, rodeo belt buckles and snake-skin boots. The womenfolk are similarly attired in tight shirts, tight shirts and cowboy boots. Most of them are on the dance floor grooving to FM radio schlock. Like Donny and Marie, they're a little bit country, a little bit rock 'n' roll; but not at all Ska. Only two locals have made any kind of effort to get into the contemporary mood. One cheeky chap has gone for a 1977 stereotype punk look, including the bondage strides, while his mate boasts an ill-fitting pork pie hat. And that's it. For the rest, it could be a day out at the rodeo. When the disco stops, the women clear the floor.

The humorous potential of the occasion isn't lost on Pauline who sets a perhaps unnecessarily sarcastic tone as soon as the band takes the stage. "Are you gonna sit down all night?" she asks, wide-eyed. "Ain't any of you Southern gentlemen got any manners? Stand up! Thank you." So not such a sweet black angel after all...

The audience is understandably bemused. They've never had a Ska band here before. The Selecter are boldly skanking where no be-crombied Brit has ever skanked before. But in fairness, in the South, we may as well be Martians. These are truly alien rhythms here. Ska was just a flash of the pan in the US, just a couple of minor hits at the turn of the last decade. Most of this lot probably think Burning Spear was a 1950s b-movie Western. And now this sassy school ma'am type, this well-spoken Romford-raised British beauty is having a pop at them for the benefit of her pals' amusement. It doesn't seem entirely wise, and even the presence of massive Cockney minder Steve English doesn't put me at ease. And yet, it works. One by one, the punters are poked, prodded and persuaded to take part of that irresistible Selecter Big Bounce, that meaty chugging beat that's welded tighter than Rod Smallwood's wallet to moving melodies and handsome hooks. The resulting colourful musical tapestry belies the band's puritanical appearance...

Pauline has always been the main draw for me, a hyper-active and heart-meltingly gorgeous Rude Girl bobbing and bopping, prancing and dancing, running on pure adrenaline with a voice, like her big bouncing breasts, that is an instrument of wonder. What's that? I shouldn't mention the breasts? You try avoiding them, pal. A lesser man would be inserting ten gallon brassiere gags into this piece with a crowbar. (Even Bette Midler was intrigued enough in LA to ask whether her strenuous activities hurt her boobs. But nay, she says. Apparently Playtex helps, but I'm too scared of her to ask.)

Pauline is as sexy as she is feisty and it'd be hypocritical not to acknowledge that most of the men in the audience would love a shot at being her Three Minute Hero.

The guy you notice most on stage is Gappa Hendricks. He's big, black and looks meaner than an Attica State Prison inmate. All through the set, Gaps stares, and snarls, and smoulders like any minute he's going to explode and tear someone's head clean off. I saw them first at the Lyceum in London last year when they'd absolutely stolen the show from the Mod headliners, demonstrating that although Secret Affair's Ian Page was right and the time was most definitely right for a new dance, it wasn't quite the one he was expecting.

In Sheffield a month later, I saw the full set – and Gappa at his most aggressive. As the band prepared to play 'Too Much Pressure' – the b-side of 'On My Radio' – you could almost see the steam coming out of his ears. Gappa let loose a stream of indecipherable Jamaican patois. "Too much bloodclaat pressure," he growled as the band lay into the meaty, beaty, big and bouncy body of the song. It was then that he decided to live up to his stage image of the kind of guy who'd use sulphuric acid for splash-on deodorant by suddenly erupting and lunging at Charley. And with Charley knocked scatty, Gaps turned and aimed himself at Desmond before hurtling back to knock smack bang into guitar star Neol.

Charley stripped off his jacket and with his immaculate six-year-old dreadlock mane flapping in unconcealed (mock) rage he steamed into his assailant reducing the stage to a sprawling mass of flying fists while, strangely oblivious to the aggro, drummer Aitch (Charles H Banbridge), keeps pounding the beat. The music never stopped.

This scene is re-enacted in Dallas. Sadly Charley's back problems mean he can't be as spirited as usual, but this is the sort of action the cowboy crowd appreciates. They whoop, they holler, they climb on chairs to stare at the unexpected aggro, a heaving sea of limbs and heads and moans and groans building to a climax where rhythm guitarist Compton is triumphantly hauled upside down and shaken silly.

It's only then, as the band immediately gets back to business, that the punters realise that we've all been party to well-acted, pre-planned frolics.

'Visually exciting' is a term readily applicable to all the 2-Tone bands and the Selecter are no exception. Live it's a case of light the blue touch paper and stand well clear. That old battleaxe Nina Myskow described their performance style as being 'stolen from a frog on pep pills.' Like the Specials, the band hailed largely from Coventry proving that the West Midlands city had more to offer than Chrysler, the Sky Blues and memories of Lady Godivá's mammaries. The original Selecter recording, on the b-side of the Specials' debut single, had all been guitarist Neol's brainchild. But by 1979 they'd become a fully-fledged gigging entity. Neol recruited the all-black reggae outfit Hard Top 22 and wooed them away from the rootsy Rasta sound that was their forte.

The Selecter share origins and ideals with the Specials, but they're not the same animal. Whereas Dammers and co mix ska and reggae with punk rock, the Selecter sound is more, as Pauline puts it "rock, reggae and soul." They're not reviving the past, they're revitalising it – using that Jamaican base to forge something new, vibrant and cross-cultural.

Neol Davies, the quiet man behind it all, shuns the limelight and modestly refuses to take the credit for Selecter's success, but it was Neol who wrote all of band's great original songs. His influences are more home-grown than you might imagine: Duane Eddy and Hank Marvin were his early guitar heroes, and The Beatles and The Who provided the sound track for his teens. Neol lived on the same Coventry street as the Specials' original drummer Silverton Hutchinson, and it was Silverton who suggested getting him in to play rock lead guitar over reggae music with Chapter 5, their band at the time. Charley Anderson recalls: "Neol rehearsed with us in the cellar a few times and performed two gigs with Chapter 5. The first one was nearly a disaster. Neol's guitar was so loud that we nearly got canned off the stage! People weren't used to it in reggae clubs." Their second gig was on the back of a truck, presumably for a quick get-away.

Recording the instrumental track 'Kingston Affair' gave Neol the idea of forming a band of his own – it was him who persuaded John Bradbury of The Specials to buy a drum kit. That band was called The Transposed Men – he took the name from a sixties comic book cover. It featured Desmond Brown on the Hammond organ, as well as Kevin Harrison (later of Urge) on guitar and Steve Wynn (later of The Swinging Cats) on bass. Neol's 'On My Radio' was the high-point of their set.

For Pauline, then known as Pauline Vickers, seeing the Foundations play at her Essex school was the first big changing point in her life. And being chatted up by them – the first black men she had ever spoken to – that made her re-think pretty much everything about herself. Adopted by a white family, she was the only non-white kid in her entire neighbourhood. She left home to find herself, discovering the joys of sex and alcohol along the way.

Pauline was studying biochemistry at Coventry University when she watched a female folk singer strumming her way through an acoustic set at the backroom folk nights in her local pub, the Old Dyer Arms pub in Spon End. Inspired, she bought herself a guitar and learnt to play it. But it wasn't until she saw Mick Jagger live that Pauline understood how to do it properly – and realised that the only way for her to enjoy performing was to go out and grab an audience by the throat. She ended up getting kicked out of the folk club for an over-enthusiastic, booze-fuelled interpretation of 'Honky-Tonk Women'.

Jazz singer Billie Holiday and Joan Armatrading were who Pauline listened to at home, though, especially winding down after her long shifts at Walsgrave Hospital where she worked as a radiologist. A local musician, a black radical called Lawton Brown realised her amazing vocal talent. They started writing songs together and he took her to see Hard Top 22. By chance, Pauline used the same rehearsal studio as the fledging Selecter. It was Lynval Golding from the Specials who spotted her talent and put Neol and Pauline together.

Neol recalls, "It was obvious she was the singer to make the songs work. It call came alive very quickly when the seven of us were together." She gratefully accepted his offer to complete the band. Last year, she turned pro, and doesn't seem to miss her old life one bit. "At the hospital, I was cleaning up balls of pus, puke and worse," she explains. "You name it, I cleaned it up. Particularly the posteriors after barium meals and enemas." So literally a shit job...

Charley Anderson, the other crowd pleaser, grew up in Montego Bay. His Mum brought him and his five siblings to the Motherland when he was eleven years old – his Dad had pissed off to the States. Seeing Jimi Hendrix on Ready, Steady, Go was all the catalyst he needed to get into music. Charley faced rejection from local kids, white and black – he was too black-skinned for the white kids, too light-skinned for the black ones.

Desmond has known him since Charley was fifteen. "Me, Charley and Lynval from the Specials used to play together in a soul band, and then we had a reggae band but we were never in to the heavy reggae, the dub side, more the uptempo stuff, the fun stuff," he says. Desmond cites his organ influences as Booker T, Jimmy Reed and perhaps more surprisingly Dave Greenfield from the Stranglers.

I first met him at Charley's humble abode in Hillfields, Coventry, after seeing the band's Sheffield gig. I'd been soaking up the atmosphere – and sifting through Chas's record collection of vintage Toots and Prince Buster singles – when Desmond decided I was a mite on the shy side and that strangulation was the best remedy. Thanks pal. Kids, do not try this at home.

The Selecter really came into their own live where most of the band work themselves into a frenzy strongly resembling a hornets' nest ten seconds after it'd been struck with a house brick, while pumping out their over-powering rhythms. Only Neol is the exception. He's happy to do little on stage, preferring to impersonate a paralysed version of the 2-Tone symbol man Walt Jabsco. 'On My Radio', a dynamic take of fickle passion and fossilised programming, was their first UK hit and 2-Tone's third...

BACK in the Bijou, the band is wearing down what's left of the audience's resistance. Pauline never leaves them alone for a moment, while Desmond deserts his Hammond to hare through them, attracting almost as many amazed stares as the "ruck 'n' roll" panto section. Incredibly the Texan punters reward them with not one, not two but three encores – a splendid 'Last Train To Skaville', a Gappa dominated 'James Bond – De Killar', and 'My Sweet Collie' (Millie's 'My Boy Lollipop' subverted into a toast to the old Bob Hope) followed by a final, fraternal rendition of 'Madness'. And that was it, the band cleared the stage, the FM disco kicked back in and then we got the Wet T-Shirt contest – various buxom blondes vying to out-do each other on the big boob/erect nipples front for a panting cluster of excitable Yanks and the despicable Halfin. I haven't seen so many wobbling chests since that Buster Bloodvessel lookalike convention.

THERE'S a lot to like about Texans. They are fiercely independent, tough, resilient, hard-working can-do people; they've got no time for anything as poncy as the welfare state and collectivism that the British have grown up with. But that I'm-all-right-Jack individualism seems to come with a side-order of "screw you" aimed at the poor and disadvantaged.

Backstage I have a beer or three with Compton, the band's 21-year-old guitarist, the son of a broken black mum/white dad home which he calls "a 2-Tone idea that didn't work." Known as Commie to his friends, he's wearing a natty suit with strides which in the true skinhead tradition look like they've just had a ruck with his shoes. A thoughtful and sensitive soul, Compton is still troubled by the band's recent day off in neighbouring Mexico. The band had visited El Paso (which translates literally as The Gateway or The Step) and slipped over the border to dirt-poor Ciudad Juarez in the Chihuahua Desert. "I couldn't get over the idea of being a tourist in other people's misery," he says. "I saw things that turned my stomach. The extreme poverty. The beggars on the street, many of them blind or deformed. Okay, we have poverty at home but to see such squalor here, right next door to oil-rich Texas – it's so disquieting, y'know."

It's a clash of values as much as anything else. As well as the 'black gold, Texas tea', Dallas is a real estate hot-bed and a bankers' paradise. In near-by Mexico, wages are low, and dropping in real value while food prices rise, benefits are virtually non-existent. There's no sign of that changing any time soon and no-one I meet in Texas seems that bothered. As one friendly taxi driver tells me, "It ain't our fault the 'Cans screwed up their economy." No sir-ee.

Compton and I chat about the Royal Rasses and Prince Lincoln Thompson's own charting of similar deprivation not too far South in 'San Salvador'. Radical dub poet Linton Kwesi Johnson, the Jamaican-born sage of Brixton, helped open Compton's eyes to political realities in his teens, he says. "He brought reggae into a British context," Commie explains. "It was music for and about black kids born in Britain and there to stay."

Black, British and proud – with music to celebrate that in a way that the old Rasta singing about Ethiopia never could. Compton is sold on every aspect of 2-Tone – the music, the ideals and the business plan. Opening the doors of a complacent pop industry to new bands and new sounds; giving talent a leg-up. Sounds punk enough to me...

NEXT morning I talk them into the ill-fated Southfork Ranch outing, which leaves us relatively subdued; reflective even. After all Dallas was the place they jeered the Sex Pistols, and killed Kennedy... and shot JR. Back on the bus, Pauline tells us about the packed, all-white truck stop that the band had managed to silence just by walking in together. When they finally got seated, the two waitresses on duty ignored them for a good fifteen minutes and, true to form, only lightened up when they realised they were English. Alf Garnett lives on this side of the pond too, only it's more than likely that here he's packing a gun.

It seems strange, not to say absurd to me, to judge people you don't know by how much melanin they have in their skin; but that, apparently, is how the world works.

For a while we travel in silence. Desmond relaxes by eating doughnuts by the dozen; the others sit back and pour over the copies of Sounds and the Daily Mirror I've brought over from England, except for Pauline who tries to lose herself in a smutty paperback, until that is Ross 'Gross Halfwit' Halfin decides to take her on. Not wise. "Why do you always look such a miserable cow in pictures?" he asks, with as much charm as a hung-over border guard with piles.

"Cos I'm a grumpy fucker," she replies equally sweetly.

Because of her medical background, the Troll brings up the subject of his genital warts. "My, you really are Gross, aren't you?" Pauline smiles, before taking the upper-hand and prodding him into purple-faced paroxysms of passion over UFO, at the time his favourite band, and our next assignment here.

"You're joking?" she scoffs. "You really enjoy heavy metal? Honestly? What, you really go to the gigs? Are you real? Can I touch you? You don't head-bang do you?"

Ross hits back with a jibe about women not liking hard rock because "you've got different brains from men...basically, a woman has got half of a man's mental capacity."

Pauline smiles. "I may have only half of your brain, dear," she says sweetly. "But I'm sure that you've only got half of what a man needs to keep a woman happy."

And with that, Pauline Black of Romford, Essex, achieves the impossible. She shuts up Ross Halfin for a good ten minutes.

SEVERAL plays of the Specials album later we arrive in Austin where the band is scheduled to do a meet-the-punters record shop stop before the gig tonight. The store stocks quality imports – even the Cockney Rejects album is here – and has been running a 'Best Rude Boy' contest with an aging Jamaican doing his Jah Russell

Harty bit over the sound system. The winner is a dim looking youth who, in the style of the old 'On My Radio' advert is clutching a battered transistor to his left lughole.

The image is ruined only by the naff shirt he's wearing, with collars like Dumbo's ear-flaps.

"What do Rude Boys do?" he asks Pauline as he picks up his prize.

Exercising remarkable self-control, she smiles sweetly and replies: "I don't know; I'm a rude girl."

"Do they smoke grass?" the youth persists; producing a skinny little spliff that looks like it wouldn't get Atom Ant high. Pauline just nods, commendably swallowing a clear desire to burst out laughing. "Cool," the kid says, and he wanders off happy.

Another guy, older and fatter with halitosis and a Buffalo Bill goatee, turns up in a strange mishmash of black and white patched clothing. He looks like a deranged Music Hall turn. And he's loud. Buffalo Bullshit. Maybe his keepers had let him out for a few minutes while they clean his cage.

"It's just another uniform here," I say, thinking out loud. "They don't get it yet." Neol Davies agrees. "Most of the country is like that. In LA especially, it's just a pose. Which is why it's good for us to play Texas, it's pretty much virgin territory."

Noel is 28, tall and ashen-faced. He describes himself as "probably the nicest person you'll ever meet." And it's probably true. Like all of the band, he has strong ideas of what The Selecter stand for. "I'm really glad that none of this band has gone to art school," he says. "I'm not making a big thing of it but I just like the idea of none of us having gone through that process. It's just a feeling I have, an earthy feel."

We talk about class, and how even racial trouble often is more to do with class and culture than ethnicity. "The middle class ideal has real power, and a lot of people aspire to it," he says. "But over here it's much worse. There's a lack of good media. On the surface the USA is about choice but when you dig deeper hardly any ideas get across at all. Even in music, it takes so long for ideas to come through. Fashions aren't really important here, whereas in England they are, as they're a way of heralding a new movement. Here everything seems to stay stuck in the past. Prejudice goes back generations here. Segregation is a tradition, a voluntary apartheid – on both sides of the racial divide. The only thing we've got like that in Britain is religion in Northern Ireland; that mule-headed sectarianism. People stay separate. There's no cultural interchange which is a real shame because I think it is people's differences that make the spark of living."

Charley Anderson is convinced the Selecter could help change that. "I think we could get across to the masses over here," the former electrical engineer says. "2-Tone isn't just a fashion. It's not a hip thing, it's a whole philosophy. We stand for people coming together socially whatever their race, creed or colour. And if we can help bridge those gaps in America, all this will have been worthwhile." Admirable sentiments indeed.

The next morning I shake hands with the band after breakfast to go off and meet up with rock legends UFO. One of the bell-boys, a friendly kid who has been smiling to all of the Selecter's faces as nice as pie, sidles up to me and grins. "You'll have a lot better time with UFO," he says. "There ain't any niggers in the band."

Postscript: The Selecter never did conquer the States, neither did they harness their remarkable live energy into a lasting studio career. Their first three singles made an impact, but subsequent releases didn't do the business. Their fourth, 'The Whisper' didn't even go Top Thirty in the UK. Increasingly pissed off, the band split from 2-Tone and decided to change direction – Charley wanted to go heavier into reggae, Neol more into rock. There were internal problems too. During the long arduous US tour, the band had split into two clear factions with Charley, Desmond, Aitch, Commie and Gaps sitting at the back of the bus smoking ganja and listening to the kind of reggae Pauline would have called misogynist. Too much pressure. Desmond quit out of the blue and for good in August, and in the resulting power struggle Charley was sacked (by Pauline) two days later. The two of them went on to form the People who never meant a light - they released one flop single and then they were gone. They were replaced by a couple of white guys from the Pharaohs. The new band slowed down the former frantic Selecter pace, softened up, aimed to be more soulful...and still flopped. They recorded a second album,

Celebrate The Bullet the following February. The title track was strong, a great atmospheric song, with addictive 'bendy' – apologies for the technical term - guitar flourishes. I loved it. At any normal time it would have been a good choice for a single, and a sure bet for the Top 20. Unfortunately it came out just weeks after John Lennon had been gunned down by Texan fantasist Mark Chapman outside of the Dakota Building in New York City. The lyrics were clearly against gun crime ('Celebrate the bullet/Put your finger on the trigger/But you don't have to pull it...') yet the title alone meant an instant radio ban. It was the band's first flop.

Poor album sales ensued.

Pauline left soon after to pursue a solo career before coming into her own on the TV where she graduated from presenting kids show Hold Tight to serious stroke dull Channel 4 chat show Black On Black. She had acting parts in TV's The Vice, Doctors and The Bill, and played Billie Holliday very well, it's said, in a stage play. She was a tough cookie – she had to be, there were very few women on the 2-Tone scene. And she remains a Ska icon; loved most of all for those first three hits and her magnificent lungs.

I've not seen Compton for thirty years, but I'm sure he would have been chuffed about the scores of quality Ska bands that erupted in Mexico. Charley Anderson and his red locks now reside in Bogota, Colombia, where he works as a producer. Various reunions and versions of the Selecter still play to this day, but largely to middle age rudies reliving their glory years. It's all retro now.

JOIN THE REJECTS, GET YOURSELF KILLED
Cockney Rejects

Custom House, East London

'I wanna get back to where it all began/I wanna do a gig in my back garden/I wanna have a laugh before the press get in/Cos if you give 'em half a chance they'll destroy the fuckin' thing'/JOIN THE REJECTS – GET YOURSELF KILLED ('Join The Rejects')

YOU want to know where Oi! started? Go to Custom House, the most run-down neighbourhood in the whole god-forsaken London borough of Newham, E16. This entire community was built around the docks; and when they closed them down there was nothing left. Nothing. You can't even rob a bank in Custom House these days because they got turned over so many times they were all shut down and boarded up.

It was here in the arse-end of the East End of London that the Cockney Rejects were born. The band was the brainchild of boxing brothers Mick and Jeff Geggus - teenage dockers' sons who re-wrote punk history. Pistols fans, they stole most of their instruments from the local music store. They thieved microphones, amps and a drum kit from their local rock venue, The Bridgehouse in Canning Town – the same venue that would later give them their first break (although they had the good sense to paint the kit a different colour when they did play there.)

They genuinely performed sets in back gardens. And they blagged and bullshitted their way into the hearts and minds of (half of) the staff of Sounds, sweet-talking me into managing them along the way. And after me and Jimmy Pursey got them a lucrative four album deal with EMI Records they gleefully stole from them as well - as detailed in Cockney Reject, the book I co-wrote with Jeff Turner.

The only things they really cared about were music and West Ham United in whose name much claret was spilt. They were like Fagin's gang, but with muscle. And a not inconsiderable Cockney charm.

I first met the two fast-talking chancers in the fabled White Lion pub in London's Covent Garden, just around the corner from the Sounds office where John Peel could often be found boozing and amusing us, and where you were far more likely to spot Phil Lynott or Buster Bloodvessel than a slumming opera star. Mick had dragged Jeff out of school to bring me their demo tape. The conversation went something like this:

Mick: "I'm Mick Geggus, this is me brother Stinky Turner. We're the Cockney Rejects. Can we give you a copy of our demo tape?"

Me: "Great name! What kind of music do you play?"

Jeff: "We're a bit like Sham."

Mick: "Yeah, Sham, Menace, UK Subs, but we've got our own sound. We ain't copied no-one."

Me: "Have you been gigging long?"

Jeff: "Only a couple of weeks" (Mick kicked him under the table) "...with this line-up."

Mick: "Yeah, just a month or so with this line-up, but loads beforehand."

Me: "Where have you played?

Jeff: "Gardens (Mick kicked him again) The Gardens, it was a little club over Silvertown way, and the Bridge House in Canning Town."

Me: "Great little venue, the Bridge House. I know the guv'nor there, Terry Murphy."

Mick (tap-dancing): "Good old Tel. Yeah we've done a bit for him."

Jeff: "We done some removals for him." (Mick shot him a look).

Mick: "We've played the Bridge, the Tidal Basin, a lot of East End venues."

Jeff: "Our following is all local. Very vocal..."

Me: How many songs you got?

Jeff: "Three..."

Mick (quickly): "Three - on that tape. We've got most of an album written. About eight numbers we're happy with an' another couple of demos..."

I KNEW there was something fishier than a trawler net full of herring about all of this, but there was something likeable and down to earth about the two young urchins too, so I offered to pass their tape on to Jimmy Pursey who was looking for bands to produce, "if it's any good." It was good, all right; very good. Very raw too, but that was part of the charm. I took the tape back and played it in the office. As soon as 'Police Car' opened up with Stinky's shout of 'Freedom? There ain't no fuckin' freedom' most of the Sounds writers cheered.

The next week, me, Dave McCullough, Robbi Millar and Eric Fuller all put the song on our playlists. I contacted Pursey, who booked them into Polydor's studios to record a proper demo. And I got them a gig at the Bridgehouse in Canning Town – their first as it turned out. Before long they had talked me into managing them, but not before I and McCullough had written this first ever Sounds feature, which was part interview and part manifesto. The original headline was 'The Cockney Rejects and the Rise of New Punk'. This is how it went...

East London, August 1979

REMEMBER when punk started? How we wanted change, how we were gonna kick out a decrepit establishment and all the Old Ways? We were supposed to be part of a working class rebellion using raw, wild, exciting rock 'n' roll music as Molotov cocktails, weren't we? WELL WEREN'T WE? 1979 and what have we got? Meet the new establishment: a Top Ten full of Tubeway Army, disco queens, and the Boomtown Prats – dramas, charmers and men in pyjamas. And ours is not to reason why, ours is just to clap and buy...IS THIS ALL WE'VE ACHIEVED?

The first wave of the new wave is washed out. Yet the critics who bucked against them now cling to their heroes just as pathetically as they did before. And the 'hippest' are the worst offenders. Even if Tony Parsons and Julie Burchill were miles wide of the mark, their book was more PUNK than Johnny Rotten playing the twat on TV's Juke Box Jury/Puke Box Spewery could ever be. THE HIPPIES HAVE TAKEN OVER AGAIN. Yeah, recreating their Pink Floyds and Genesises and ELPs in the hallowed name of progress. Good ideas like Rock Against Racism have ended up a 'nice', 'liberal' cul-de-sac for nursery school lefties.

Y'know what the legacy of three years of 'political awareness' is? A couple of hundred human hand-grenades storm-trooping in a stupor around gigs in the name of something as hideous, pathetic and anti-working class as Nazism. While the dated, ineffective out-to-lunch Left might as well be speaking Latin – and "Let's have a meeting about the sexuality of Argentinean lumpen-proletarian revisionists, Maurice..." FUCK OFF!

'Punk Rockers' in hand-me-down images play at being rebels, as if bondage pants and mascara around your baby blues mean anything anymore. Tell us, what's the difference between you and some lump in denim flares and Yes sew-on patches? IT'S A JOKE, PAL. A FARCE. And all 'the stars', 'our heroes', the 'kids off the street' all turned out to be phoney baloneys. As Billy Idol told the Daily Mirror three weeks ago: "Actually I had a nice middle class upbringing." It's safe to tell the truth now. The working class can kiss my arse, I've got the pop star job at last...DID YOU EVER FEEL BETRAYED?

"Betrayed? Of course I feel betrayed. It's like everything has gone back to what it was like in '74 and '75, but I honestly think it's started back again in the East End. The feeling's coming back again..."

Micky Geggus is 18. Up until a few months ago he was a promising amateur boxer on the verge of turning pro. He'd never been put down in the ring and a bright future seemed assured. Micky is now on the dole, and he's none too proud of the fact. The reason he puts up with something that is considered a serious social stigma in his family is his concern for the band in which he plays guitar and co-pens some furious lyrics. The band are the Cockney Rejects, four tousle-haired wide boys from East London's forgotten dockland area of Custom House.

The reason the Rejects are featured in this intemperate outburst of ours is strictly their own doing. Since Bushell received and went bananas over a tape of the band's 'Police Car' and other songs, the Rejects have fought their way into the life of Sounds.

The tape is pure brutal reality. Next to the crooning dark emperors of (ho ho) the new 'alternative' cultures, the fad-fuckers of today, these boys sound like The Truth. They also sound aggrieved, and then some.

The Rejects are Micky, his 15-year-old younger brother Stink Turner on vocals, drummer Geoff Wilmott and bassist Big Vince Riordan. But to start with they were Micky and Stinky. Mick got his first guitar in the 'God Save The Queen' summer of 1977 and a series of minor endeavours ensued. As The Shitters, he and Stinky played various gigs in back gardens, parks and mate's houses; anywhere really. The Rejects are a more serious endeavour and the current line-up has been in existence for only a week, so they had a different drummer and bassist on their Small Wonder spit-and-guts ep released last week.

Vince used to play guitar with the Dead Flowers. He also spent over a year as a roadie for Sham 69, an experience that left him disillusioned as we shall see. Wilmott is late of the Corvettes and joined the band after their Bridgehouse debut. That night Andy Scott, formerly of The Tickets, sat in on drums. It was a gig that despite Vince's virginal nerves firmly demonstrated that the Rejects' live sound lives up to their studio promise: the music tough and hard, the words unforgiving. An out and out new punk assault. A right kick up the Khyber.

"But that's what punk should be," Micky explodes. "It should be bands like us. It should be raucous and a fuckin' big shout and a bang in the mouth."

DON'T get the idea they're just violent head-cases though. Sure they can look after themselves, Vince spent months protecting Sham 69 along with Binnsy, the Rejects roadie. Stinky has also given up a promising boxing career – he's boxed for England and like Mick has never been put down in the ring. But they're not bullies. "We are what people thought Sham were," Micky explains.

"We are just four East Enders, you won't find another band as real as us or who mean it like us." So when you hear Stinky roar "Freedom? They're ain't no fuckin' freedom" you won't be surprised to learn that he's up before the beak in two month's time after getting nicked on the terraces at West Ham for alleged threatening behaviour – a charge he denies.

The group's pivotal members – Mick, Jeff and Vince – are charismatic characters who each have a lot to say. Approved school graduate Vince looks as though he's spent his early years on Alcatraz eating gorillas for breakfast. He's also witty and incorrigibly funny. Micky talks as fast as Vince drinks and Stinky's a young nutter with a gap in his teeth like the Blackwall Tunnel. Admittedly they're hard – they don't need an A-Z to learn about the streets, man. But they're also humane as befits people from good East London Labour-voting families, with an honest dislike of any authority which puts them down, including NF/BM fascists.

"See it ain't the police we're against as such," explains Micky. "Because as said Mensi there's no-one I respect more than an honest copper, but I tell ya they're a dying breed. There is so much abuse of power it's untrue."

'They put me in a cell/With a load of drunks as well/And I can still remember, that awful pissy smell...' ('They're Gonna Put Me Away')

"My old man's a docker, he's been a docker all his life," says Mick. "And he looks at me as the laziest cunt going cos I ain't got a job since I got the sack from Newham Council. But I don't wanna get up at seven every morning and get home at five for the rest of me life so everyone can say what a good bloke I was. I wanna achieve something."

"There's only three ways out of the East End – boxing, football and rock 'n' roll," says Vince, neglecting to add the fourth exit route, a coffin.

"I believe we're gonna make it," Mick says. "I really do believe in this band. Now it's a perfect mix of me and Stinky's enthusiasm and Vince and Binnsy's experience because they are geezers who about rock 'n' roll first hand and know all about posers."

The band have nothing but contempt for punk rock 'stars': The Banshees, Strummer, even Pursey. "I'll tell you what, he shit on us and he shit on Sham 69," Vince explodes. "He uses people. He used us. When there were rows after a gig, he'd be out the back and we'd be left to face the music."

The Rejects go on stage with a huge home-made banner boasting West Ham's crossed hammers, a Union Jack and the words 'West Side' referring to part of the Upton Park terraces. Aren't they worried about getting Sham's sort of heavy, violent head-case following?

"Nah," says Micky. "Okay, we'll get a hard following but no harder than the band."

"See, we can handle it," Binnsy explains. "We're the same as them, and we can talk to them. If they want a row we'll have a row. Pursey couldn't do that."

'There ain't gonna be no argument/There ain't gonna be no sentiment/I don't like what you just said/Now I'm gonna bash your head...' ('Ready To Ruck').

"I don't want you to get the idea that we're a violent band though," says Mick. "I mean you take the song 'Ready To Ruck', now that is a piss-take of the way it is round our way, where geezers will fight just for looking at each other. It's so pointless that sort of thing."

AT the moment their only hardcore followers are Stinky's mates, around thirty teenagers organised into a gang called the Rubber Glove Firm. But each gig brings more and more support, and grudging respect because even cynics can recognise that this band have all the spirit of punk as well as being one of the few real groups in existence. We can see them getting a huge following.

"It's something that worries me," Mick confesses. "Cos I wanna be a star, sure I do. I wanna be on Top Of The Pops. But I don't wanna shit out. All we've done is swap our cloth caps for leather jackets and I know I don't ever wanna change. We're just working class blokes given a chance to have our say and we're gonna take it. But I don't buy all this stuff tossers like Crass say about the Clash dying when they signed to CBS. If they hadn't signed I'd never have heard of them. We need a deal, we need the money; we need a back line. We need gear and a van. At the moment we're borrowing gear from mates."

But you're going to get ripped off by record companies, aren't you?

Vince clenches his fist. "That would give me the good pleasure of smacking someone in the mouth," he says. "And I ain't saying that because I'm trying to be tough. We're not gonna take no bollocks. If anyone tries to change us, that's what they'll get."

***

Within a year, the Cockney Rejects had notched up hit singles and a well-received debut album. But their passion for West Ham and their allegiance to the ICF attracted many enemies. In June 1980, their show at the Cedar Club in Birmingham witnessed the worst gig violence ever seen in Britain – which I have written about at length in my book Hoolies. I likened it to the rock 'n' roll equivalent of Rorke's Drift. The bloody fighting, destruction and subsequent court cases ended the Rejects' career as a touring band for more than twenty years.

DON'T FUCK WITH THE BALDIES!
Bad Manners

June 1980, Scotland

"You won't print this will you? Well I had diarrhoea for two days and – you promise not to print this? – remember that white boiler suit I used to have? Well I was wearing it when I had to make a run for the bog. Except someone was in there, and..." – Doug Trendle.

I'm on the cramped Bad Manners tour bus, somewhere in the east of Scotland. It could be the low road, it could be the high road, there's no way of telling. The humour is low; the behaviour most definitely suggests high. This battered old van must be going close on 60mph and yet half of the merry mob of oddballs I'm travelling with insist on climbing out of the window and swinging up onto the roof rack.

What a bunch of ne-ne-na-na-na-na-nutters!

If that's not bad enough, in front of me Winston Bazoomies, the tousle-haired harmonica player, is swinging around like a demented gibbon with a clapped-out cassette player pinned to his left ear. It's blasting out the most eccentric mix of music this side of the Peel show: a chronic smorgasbord of sonic insanities ranging from Cajun pop to rasta-beat via Irish jigs, Creole zydeco and what sounds like Greek rockabilly – kebababilly? – that has lost its (Elgin) marbles.

"This is pirate music," he hollers. "Ahhh! Sing lad, Jim lad."

He falls to the floor like a pole-axed ox, ripping his shirt in the process, but keeps on yelping, "C'mon boys, are you ready? Here we goooo!"

"He's been like this since he was four years old," explains beefy Buster Bloodvessel, alias the equally beefy Doug Trendle, patiently. "He couldn't speak properly until he was about ten. He used to wander around Hackney saying things like, 'Papa beat me, and I have to go home for my tea', and 'Give me your false teeth and I'll eat your jaw.' He used to feed his sister leaves.

"One day me and my best mate, Eric Delaney, bowled round his house and found him screwing his mattress, literally! No lie." Let's hope at least that it was well upholstered...and open coil. Doug pauses as if to consider the image, and then adds poetically "If sperm were rocket fuel, that mattress would have flown like an Arabian carpet."

Winston is of course the man who delivers the three minute gibberish intro over the Magnificent Seven theme at the start of the band's set. The trouble is his lunacy is not confined to the stage. Already on this tour he's got the Bad lads and sometime tour support, Ska band Headline, ejected from a motorway cafe in Cornwall for giving a demonstration recital on top of a table. And he has frequently got them all ejected from warm guest house beds thanks to his odd habit of screaming "the world's loudest yelp" at unexpected moments.

Bazoomies seems to have crossed the line between eccentric and down-right section-able.

BAD Manners main man (mountain) Doug is firmly on the showbiz side of crazy, though. The guy is so bald you can practically read his mind, and so fat he could moon Glasgow...and he uses these physical attributes for maximum effect. Not least his thirteen inch conger eel of a tongue, which takes, or rather gives, some licking, eh girls? Most of the printable stuff involves challenges. Largely they're food and drink related, however backstage at Tiffany's in Edinburgh, I feel obliged to tip him off about another challenge being issued this week by the Jaws column in Sounds inviting his alter ego Buster Bloodvessel to rassle someone in a proper wrestling ring; that someone being professional grapple giant Big Daddy, a man whose 24stones make Buster seem almost slim.

Doug, who is a mere 18stone ("nineteen with me steel-caps on"), isn't even phased. "I'll take him on if he's getting flash," Britain's biggest Ska star retorts instantly. "It is a bit worrying I suppose, he makes me look like Twiggy. But I'll wear me steels. He won't stand a chance. I doubt if he'll even turn up. Madness never did..."

Doug is of course referring to the ever-postponed Madness versus Bad Manners rugby match. "Madness can't get it together," he says, dismissively. "They reckon they're too busy touring, but it would have happened if they'd wanted it to happen. If you ask me they shit themselves when they found out we had three players who used to play for Middlesex and one who played for Kent County in the band. Suggsy in a scrum? Don't make me laugh."

Gene Simmons from Kiss never responded to that tongue measuring challenge either, did he? I say, stirring like Fanny Craddock on piece-rate. "Nah, he's another one who bottled out," Doug sighs. "But I'd meet him any day. See, I reckon his tongue is probably longer than mine but it ain't as thick or as wide and I don't reckon he can move it at all, all he can do is stick it out. Not only is my tongue stronger but also I can do ballet with it. Look."

Without pausing to draw breath Doug pokes out his ferocious fleshy organ and gives a dazzling display: Coppélia, Swan Lake, Cinderella, A Midsummer's Night Dream, and an eye-watering Nutcracker...it's magical. He does it all, pirouettes, glissades, pas de seul, pas de basque – his mastery of oral choreography is beyond dispute. If that tongue could talk what a cunning linguist it would be.

Yep, I'd wager that Douglas would whip the arse of the flash septic Simmons with the same ease with which he beat Judge Dread in the recent Battle of the Bulges in Sounds the other week. ("And Dread wore padded y-fronts for that," Doug divulges in mock horror).

But of course the most effortless challenge of them all is the one Buster takes on in every performance with the band – turning a club full of passive punters into a sea of happy skankers.

At Edinburgh, the Tartan tickets aren't slow to succumb to those dance-happy Ska 'n' b rhythms...

BACK-TRACK several months to my first encounter with these lunatics. I was staying at a hotel in Coventry when this ginormous geezer rolled in wearing a shabby old crombie over-coat. The fat man had a ridiculous looking natty dread hat on his head that looked like John Bindon's willie warmer, and a great big cherubic smile on his face. It was of course Dougie Trendle (born Douglas Woods). He strolled up to the pretty brunette behind the reception desk, winked, and, as bold as brass asked her "Would you like to come and see a band with a hit single tonight?"

"What's it called?" she asked, understandably suspicious. Doug took one step back, stuck out his massive chest and roared "NE-NE-NA-NA-NA-NA-NU-NU" at full volume. Then he stuck out his titanic tongue and pulled off the silly hat to reveal a bonce shaved as bald as a billiard ball. Everyone in the reception area dissolves into hysterics. The fat man turned and left the hotel, squelching his folds of quivering flab into a waiting taxi.

"Where was the gig?" I asked the girl behind the desk, when she'd stopped giggling.

"Warwick University," she replied, and starting tittering fit to burst again.

I had to see this. I jumped in a cab to the venue, talked my way backstage, and found a door with a sign on it which read simply 'Bad Manners – Keep Out.' How pleasant. But I was far too intrigued to stop now. I walked right in and regretted it immediately. The fat man was there with his eight other band members standing in a ragged semi-circle chanting nonsense. They waved their hands and patted their brows; they groaned, they grinned, they grimaced and they war-danced. It was horrific, blood-chilling; like a New Zealand rugby haka performed by the Goons. The colour drained from my face. Gentle reader, I had witnessed something few men will ever see: the Bad Manners pre-gig warm-up ritual.

Then they pushed me aside and made straight for the stage. Buster stayed out of sight while the eight other loonies launched into a rich and brassily beefy Ska arrangement of the Magnificent Seven theme. That was my first experience of seeing Bazoomies acting like a man vaccinated with a gramophone needle dipped in mescaline. He stood there shaking and trembling as he mumbled incomprehensible nonsense into the microphone until Buster bowled on from stage left to roar: "SHADDUP!"

Eleven slices of luscious lunacy followed, intoxicatingly enjoyable enough to suggest that despite this being as late in the 2-Tone day as March 1980 and despite various smug pundits already talking dismissively about a "2-Tone bandwagon" and "worthless cash-in bands", Bad Manners were something a little bit special; real prospects.

Buster was inevitably the visual mainstay throughout the live performance, screwing up his face into agonies of anguish while toasting like a nutcase, pouring beer over his noggin, alternatively thrusting out his gigantic belly and revolting tongue at the crowd. But Buster also hit the only bum note here tonight, though, because at this stage of the band's career he was wont to periodically drop his jeans and flash the biggest and most disgusting arsehole you've ever seen at the blissfully skanking punters. Talk about Moon Over Miami, mes amis.

His chief rival for the eye-balls was the aforementioned Winston Bazoomies (born Alan Sayag), who would never stop moving, swinging his head and shoulders about with such jerky force that he was always threatening to shed his silly yellow sunglasses. Behind him was the more sober looking keyboard player Martin Stewart in his shirt and tie. Stewart, a hardy Scot, purported to be a former shepherd which possibly explains why the band's Hackney-born black drummer Brian Chew-It (actually Tuitt) always used to give him those worried sideways glances.

Then there was the brass section: Birmingham boy Andrew 'Marcus Absent' Marson (sax), willowy Gerry Cottle's Circus veteran Chris Kane (sax) and stocky trumpet tooter Gus 'Hot Lips' Herman. And that just left elfin bass player Reggie Mental, known to his parents as David Farren, and last but not prettiest, guitarist Louis 'Alphonso' Cook to complete the set. Louis always looked like he should be playing a banjo in Deliverance. He was more of a country bumpkin than a dapper Rude Boy, and had the strange habits associated with his kind. One Halloween night he broke into a coffin at Highgate Cemetery, pulled out a skull by its hair, and had a game of football with it... an image that brings a tear to the eye, not least of the poor desecrated corpse.

THE Bad Manners story begins with Buster. He was born on 6th September 1958 to single mother Lillian Wood in Hackney, East London, and although obviously he never went hungry, there was never much money about. The young Doug was adopted and raised by his great aunt Mary Trendle and her husband Edward – something he discovered by accident when over-hearing a conversation when he was seven. He had known his real Mum as

Auntie Lilly, but he never knew his father (believed by many to have been the Michelin Man).

Doug started his musical career on the Arsenal North Bank, as a keen purveyor of football chants. His first official performance was in front of a magistrate after getting collared for "obscene singing" at QPR's ground. The doddery old Barnaby Rudge asked for a recital and even he had to laugh when "Who the fuck is Stanley Bowles?" wafted back full blast across the courtroom.

Former plumber Doug formed the first line-up of Bad Manners at Woodberry Down comprehensive school in Manor House, North London in 1976. They originally called themselves Stoop Solo and the Sheet Starchers. But they didn't start playing seriously until the summer of 1978. Over the next twelve months the Manners gang developed a style of their own. Like Madness, Manners were always more into fun and games and having a laugh than they were on social comment. Their chief distinguishing quality was an old-school rhythm and blues tinge, as exemplified by their Ska-ed up version of Sam the Sham's old 12-bar classic 'Wooly Bully' – a Pharoah hit for the Texan combo back in 1965. Which explains how they came to brand their music Ska'n'B. It was never particularly accurate, as the R'n'B was only evident in a couple of the songs they played. In reality, the Manners mainstays have always been big visual fun, the carnival brass sound, and a superlative blend of old Trojan favourites such as 'Elizabethan Reggae' and 'Double Barrel' which they interspersed with their own Ska-pop smashes. It was a mix that appealed to all sorts of audiences from skinheads to rugby clubs via pissed-up students.

Jerry Dammers saw them live in London in 1979, at about the same time as he first clocked Madness, and was impressed enough to offer them a deal with 2-Tone. It was probably sensible, in retrospect that they turned him down. By signing with Magnet, no-one could realistically accuse Bad Manners of riding the 2-Tone bandwagon. The band's debut single, that great Mork from Ork reminiscent mutation 'Ne-Ne Na-Na' scraped into the Top Thirty in March, peaking at 28; and the follow-up 45 'Lip Up Fatty' made it to No.15 in the summer. It would take their third single, 'Special Brew', Buster's moving love song to tramp-strength lager, to finally get the Manners boys into the Top Three where they belonged in September.

Back in Scotland, I watched the band demolish another audience's resistance. But as Bad Manners take the stage I'm surprised to notice a sudden outbreak of cropped haircuts among their ranks, with Alphonso, Hot Lips and Brian Chew-It all sporting shaven domes to match Buster's own. It makes the whole crew look like an off-shoot of the blubbery Fordham Baldies clan from hit US movie The Wanderers – especially when they are joined on stage by Bongo and the boys from the local skinhead battalion. The film's man mountain Terror (surely Doug's long-lost evil twin?) would have noted with approval that no-one "fucked wid da Baldies" this night. And a few music press pseuds would have been horrified to see even Hilary from 'cred' post-punk The Flowers dancing blissfully in the audience to the Manners' heavy heavy Munster sound. A good 250 happy punters were carried along by the "tatty tinkle of rude boy muzak" ((c) Dave McCullough) for an exhaustingly good eighteen song session.

The next morning, Martin Stewart takes over the van wheel for a hazardous drive to Aberdeen. I take shelter in the back with Doug and his pretty but petite girlfriend (again reminiscent of Terror's Tiny) who, at a humble seven stone 10lbs, inspires no end of unsavoury speculation about their sex life. Girl, you've got to carry that weight a long time...

As hipflasks of Scotch and spliffs circulate, Douglas suggests I partake of a little gentleman's snuff. Sadly it's not Peruvian in origin; but merely pulverised tobacco leaves for the snorting of. He proffers a box marked JH Wilson's Medicated Snuff for my perusal.

"It's very invigorating," he tells me, shortly before I sample it and then collapse, nostrils stinging, in a violent and protracted sneezing fit. "It clears the nose out, and it's really refreshing, don't you reckon?" My reply, mumbled and groaned from the floor of the van, is mercifully drowned out by a fresh blast of pirate music. But I think the word skanker was in there somewhere.

Unabashed, Doug relates some of the even more stomach-churning tour stories to date – confirming reports of a shotgun attack on their support band Headline at St Austell. "Yeah, luckily the bullet exploded in one of the suitcases," he says. "It just missed the keyboardist's head." The attack was apparently motiveless and the lunatic responsible has been charged.

Less seriously, Doug suffered a nasty attack of food poisoning at Bridlington after polishing off a "bad crab whole." I wasn't even aware crabs had holes, but you learn something every day. The resulting 48 hour onslaught of the leaping Leon Trotskies is referred to in the quote at the beginning of this article. The boiler suit has since been burned, and its ashes scattered to the four winds.

Pausing only to salute the Bell's distillery as we pass, we pull off the main drag to visit Auchtermuchty, a quiet town in Fife made famous by John Junor's column in the Sunday Express as a bastion of ordinary opinion and sensible god-fearing reactionary folk. The stern no-nonsense Junor would certainly have invited Alice to pass her sick-bag if he'd known that keyboardist Martin Stewart had spent his formative years here allegedly "sheep-shagging" (D. Trendle) or perhaps more accurately shepherding for an elderly lady farmer.

We drop in for a refreshing eight pint breather in Martin's old local, the Boar's Head, where various family members have turned up to meet the band. While they make small talk, I take the opportunity to elicit all the boring old Actual Information that music paper articles are full of. This short Scottish stint includes a performance at the Loch Lomond festival; after that Bad Manners team up with Headline again to finish off the English tour dates. Next month they play a Finnish fest alongside Iron Maiden in front of 50,000 punters, which should be quite a laugh, proving Buster doesn't eat Eddie or vice versa.

Their debut album Ska 'N' B came out in April and has gone silver. They're planning to record the follow-up, 'Loonee Tunes' in July for a pre-Christmas release; this is likely to include a couple of the live covers left over from the first album, like 'Tequila' and 'El Pussycat' as well as the expected bold and brassy originals. I raise the subject of possible musical progression which provokes a Buster-sized ruck between Doug and Bazoomies. Doug reckons they should move more towards "big band Ska" (sort of Laurel Aitken meets Billy Cotton at the Stoke Newington pie shop). The barking mad Bazoomies argues passionately in favour of swinging towards Cajun and general "pirate music". "You're talking out of your Arrrs," says Doug poetically.

Just to confuse matters further, Mr Alphonso puts forward an alternative scheme of doing a nine album long Ska interpretation of Wagner's Ring Cycle which would probably see them through until pension time; although knowing Doug he'd probably get stuck up, sorry, on Brunnhilde.

Out of the blue, a boozy Buster starts babbling on about an alleged "world anti-flab conspiracy", muttering darkly about the way Hollywood insists on hiring nice, slender heroes while baddies are generally portrayed by the over-weight. It's all a bit too predictable, so I'll interrupt his flow with a few amazing Bad Manners facts. Such as:

-Their debut single 'Ne-Ne Na-Na' was not inspired by Mork from Ork's "Nanoo Nanoo" at all, but is actually a cover of an obscure number by a 1950s US combo called Dickie Doo & The Don'ts (actually the work of producer Gerry Granahan).

-Doug nicked his stage name Buster Bloodvessel from the bus conductor character played by Ivor Cutler in the Beatles' 1967 film Magical Mystery Tour.

-The band's rotund roadie Roy spends much of his spare time taping smutty stories from porn mags which he brings on tour as, ahem, educational entertainment.

-And Brian 'Chew-It' Tuitt has a thing about fish and little Asian women but, over-all, if pushed, would opt for little Asian fish.

There is a lot more in this vein which it's probably best not to bother about. My note book from this tour includes progressively sillier nonsense from Bazoomies where he claims to have been an ant called Cedric in a former life, and rambles on about his next door neighbour painting his front door with a feather; but if you think the details are worth including you are probably as crazy as he is.

Back on the van, Doug talks at length about his hero Judge Dread, and his memories of skins years before at the Tottenham Royal (of 'Saturday Night Beneath The Plastic Palm Trees' fame – "dancing to the rhythms of the 'Guns Of Navarone"); the whole

101

fascinating conflab stopping prematurely when stern Sounds snapper Virginia 'Fleshy Parts' Turbett insists on stopping the van for what feels like a ten hour photo session. This ends with saxophonist (and Harold Wilson sound-alike) Chris Kane getting hurled fully clothed into a lake.

"Don't worry Gal," roars Doug from inside a clump of ferns. "Next time we see you we'll have something serious to say about the state of the world as it is today, honest we will..."

Next time? NEXT TIME? AAAAAARRRGGGHHHHHHHH!

Postscript: THERE were several next times of course, but the one I wish I could remember more clearly was my trip to Germany with the lads almost exactly one year later. I can recall going to Hamburg with them, and Doug taking me along to his favourite Reeperbahn knocking shop (called Crazy Sexy) in St Pauli, the details of which are perhaps best left unreported – much as a certain 'double oral' incident involving biker girls and chocolate sauce in Sheffield will be...as long as his cheque clears. Although I do like the fact that the German for bunk-up is bumpsen and when Hans needs the bumpsen Daisy, he knows exactly where to go to unburden his bratwurst...

I also recall Doug and the band breaking out into a terrace chant of "Two world wars and one world cup, England! England!" and the whole lot of us having to run what felt like the entire length of die sündige Meile (the sinful mile) to escape the wrath of locals who spoke English much better than we sprechened Deutsche. The cops were involved but we still got to the gig in time – a huge open air festival with the Bad lads supporting the far more restrained quirky pop band Fischer-Z in Stadt Park. The lucky Krauts got to savour three brand new Manners masterpieces, all as breezy as a winter's day on the Russian front, but none better received than the new single 'Can Can'.

The best thing about the resulting two page spread in Sounds was that it came with artwork by Curt Vile better known to the world now as the genius Alan Moore of 'Watchmen', 'Swamp Thing' and 'V For Vendetta' fame. To the best of my recollection, Alan/Curt only did three of these spreads – one for Bad Manners, one for Saxon and the third for the Cockney Rejects. The Manners one was headlined 'The Deranged Doings of Desperate Doug...and his demented droogs!' It was basically a picture spread, with my captions, and Curt's graphics across the top. They were in British comic book style, with caricatures of the band, a running bottle of Special Brew, walking hamburgers, a guest appearance by Desperate Dan, and Buster in an unsoiled boiler suit carrying a particularly sexy, tackled-up 'Lorraine' under his arms. The original artwork is probably worth thousands now, and sadly it's as lost as Paradise.

The hits would keep coming for the world's maddest musical misfits at least for another couple of years. They released twelve singles of which only one, 1983's 'Samson & Delilah' failed to go Top 50. They had four Top Ten chart-busters – that summer's 'Can Can' went Top Three; 1982's 'My Girl Lollipop' (a gender reassigned version of Millie's 'My Boy Lollipop') peaked at No.9 – and six more top forty hits. Two of their first five albums went Top 30, three of them going silver.

In fact the only serious set-backs in the band's golden age were on the challenge front.

Doug was more than a little perturbed when some appalling health-obsessed quack made him abandon his greatest endurance test to date – eating more than 27 Big Macs (his record) in one sitting.

When word of that got out, Doug's reputation wobbled like his formidable gut. "Sod the doctors," he told me angrily. "The doctors told me to stop the eating contests but I'm going to have to keep on, just to keep my head above water.

"You know I met Chrissy Boy out of Madness in Stockholm and even he challenged me to an eating contest. I mean, Chrissy Boy!"

It was a shocker. And there was another one coming when Winston Bazoomies took on Chas Smash in a little-reported nuttiness joust which, although judged to be "a terrifying stalemate", left Bazoomies apparently "traumatized" and unable to tour. (Although thinking about, it that may just have been a PR story to cover the lovable lunatic leaving the band.) At least Doug finally met Big Daddy, although to the best of my knowledge the actual bout didn't take place before the giant wrestling star, whose real name was Shirley Crabtree, died in 1997.

Bad Manners were always my favourite live Ska band. They turned every show in to a party. But my funniest memory from those early Munsterous Manners months came when Doug and I were sitting in a hotel restaurant one evening in 1980. It was a rather plush place, full of snobs, but Doug couldn't care less. He took off his battered old black crombie to reveal a thick white sweater riding up over several spare tyres, themselves exposed to the world through a shirt riddled with holes the size of soccer balls.

Unsurprisingly the waitress couldn't stop herself from bursting out laughing. Finally, after several minutes of uncontrollable giggling she said, "Excuse me sir, would you like anything off of the sweet trolley?"

"No ta," Doug replied straight-faced. "It's fattening."

Priceless.

"What if your Mum could see you now," I asked him.

"You're joking," Dougie replied aghast. "She don't even know I'm in a band. She'd kill me. Nah, she thinks I'm working on a building site..."

And off he went back to the bar for another can of Special Brew, poking his tongue out at the toffee-nosed diners and wobbling ferociously. Let's face it, after all of that he just had to be a star.

BLEED FOR YOU
The Ruts

Exeter, June 1979

IT was all going so well too, that was the point. So everyone assumed it was part of the act. I must admit I was a bit surprised, having seen the Ruts a fair few times without witnessing so much as a sprained pinkie, but here we are halfway through their set in Exeter's Routes Club and Malcolm Owen is starting to look like Chuck Wepner at the end of round seven of his catastrophic clash with Sonny Liston. The singer's forehead is gushing blood.

The Ruts were halfway through 'It Was Cold', a comparatively slow, atmospheric number, when Malcolm began banging his noggin on Dave Ruffy's cymbals. He then staggered back to his microphone. Now the claret is spurting like a miniature fountain. Much more of this and he'll be getting fan mail from Victoria Falls.

So he thinks he's Iggy Pop or what? A few of us in the crowd start to worry. Malc looks as stunned as a drunken bum whose sleep under the Charing Cross arches has been disturbed by the sudden arrival of Eamonn Andrews and his big red book. But the image ties in so well with the music we think it must be part of the act. He's play-acting, right?

Then Malcolm gobs absent-mindedly and grabs the mic. "Look," a West Country voice roars. "Ee's spitting now – ee's alright, me luvvers." The crowd respond in kind and Malc's jet black dicky-dirt is swiftly smothered with great pustules of phlegm that mix with the freshly spilt corpuscles into a sickly blend that drips down onto his Hampton-hugging blue jeans (Mr Humphries writes). His arms hang as loose as his braces that dangle by his left knee-cap.

As the song ends, Malcolm winds down towards the floor in perfect synch – see, told you it was part of the act – then he springs back to his feet before collapsing again like the proverbial pole-axed ferret. HEY, he is hurt, ain't somebody gonna...

Wide-boy manager Andy Dayman takes control and he and Segs rush the fallen singer away by ambulance to Devon & Exeter Hospital for what turns out to be a nine stitches job. He'd lost two pints of blood. Segs reckons Malcolm spent the journey claiming not to know who Andy was. Back at the gigs, the Damned dedicated 'Stretcher Case' to him.

Later Malcolm tells me he didn't even know he was bleeding. He was so out of it he thought it was sweat! He blames a mix of post-flu antibiotics and alcohol, which go together like Captain Hook and child care; although with the benefit of hindsight, we can be pretty sure the "medicine" was more likely to have been opium-based.

It certainly wasn't anything as crass (or safe) as a publicity stunt...

THE RUTS came together one easy summer day when the two sevens were rashly clashing. They were Malcolm (now 24, he claims) vocals, ex-postman John Jennings (AKA Vince Segs; now 23), bass, genial drummer Dave Ruffy (now 25) who used to work in the fabrics department of a department store, and old lag of the band guitarist Paul Fox, an ex-labourer (now the grand old age of 28) who appears to be breaking in a haircut for Bad Company.

None of them had particularly prestigious pedigrees. Foxy and Dave had previously, performed in a nine-piece local circuit funk outfit called Hit And Run, Segsy ("the lowest of the low") was a H&R roadie, while Malcy had left school at 15 for six months as a tool maker before slipping into fronting bands and after flogging TV sets in an electrical store developed an usual line in freelance enterprise (drug-dealing.)

They worked like coolies, gigging relentlessly for their first sixteen months. Many of those shows were Rock Against Racism jobs in the suburbs of West London with Southall-based reggae band Misty In Roots (thus the Ruts are known as "a Southall band" even though Dave and Segs grew up in East London and live in Forest Hill, South London, and Paddington-born Foxy resides in Northwood, which is up by the Hertfordshire border).

This year they've gone from relative obscurity to the brink of national break-through recognition with a Top Of The Pops slot in the near future I'd wager. In January their first single 'In A Rut'/'H Eyes' came out on the People Unite Southall co-op label and reached 82 in the national chart, selling over 20,000 copies and paving the way for two Peel sessions, a Kid Jensen session, and a signing with Virgin in April. Not bad considering it only set them back a measly £105quid to record.

Last week their blisteringly brilliant second single 'Babylon's Burning' set off on its chart-bound course with a Ruts album scheduled to be recorded in July and released this September. Seems their future is looking brighter than a Mastermind winner on a tanning bed.

EXETER Routes club before the aforementioned ugly incident is no exception, with the eight numbers they manage to complete giving ample evidence of the band's scope and strength. Their set romps from the full-frontal, paranoia-fuelled power-punk assault of 'Society' through the relatively restrained menacing rock atmospherics of 'S.U.S.' to the stabbing guitar and reggae vibe of the newest number 'Jah War' written about April's violent anti-National Front protest in Southall (of which, more later).

Just for the crack I hang about for the endearingly atrocious Aunty Pus and a hugely enjoyable if chaotic account of cranked up really high punk vaudeville from the dear old Damned and then head back to the hotel with ace snapper Virginia Turbett and Dave from the label. I can't remember the name, that's not my Forte, but it was definitely more doss-house than Dorchester.

Gloriously, the low-rent establishment makes Fawlty Towers seem as sane as the Savoy and as posh as the Ritz. First off there's Cyril, the "I heard that, pardon?" night porter, star of such exchanges as:

"Four cheese sandwiches."

"What sort of damages?"

And "On the tab"

"Order a cab? Where to, sir?"

Then there's the wild-eyed acid casualty on crutches who follows everyone about demanding to know where the party is...

The party, if you can call it that, is eventually located in Malcolm and Segs' bijou room. I find Malc nursing his stitches, and Segs telling of previous encounters with the hotel's resident trip enthusiast over assorted sandwiches and gratefully assaulted lagers. I chat with Foxy about our mutual idol, Hendrix. Then dapper Dave turns up in his red coat and tries to organise nobbly knee contests (Rutlins! There's a thought. A few of us would settle for a glamorous punk rock granny at this juncture).

Sad to say, your intrepid reporter is not at his best tonight as I'm suffering from Man Flu (women just don't get it). The interview will have to wait until tomorrow, I explain. Apart from some unsavoury comments about "dual-purpose tissues", everyone is sympathetic and I retire early to my bed to drift into the arms of Morpheus.

SUCH a nice bunch of lads the Ruts; rather than wait to see how I am in the morning, the sniggering gits persuade the dithering night porter to lead them into my bedroom for a chaotic 3am raid.

All I can recall is calling them all 'see you next Tuesdays' in a loving and caring way and waking up at nine with a lampshade on my head.

Over breakfast the wretched Segs explains they'd been looking for his escaped woollen budgie Baama (a creature possessed of legendary powers far too obscene for family reading). Unimpressed, I arrange to meet 'em back in London at 2.30pm for the interview proper. Naturally this is a mistake. They eventually hit Covent Garden two hours late. I'd popped out for some fresh air/lager, and find Malcolm collapsed in a crumpled heap of failed humanity outside the office doors, while Foxy leads the others in obscure boozing songs. A backseat littered with more drained scrumpy bottles than a Wurzels dressing room tells me everything I need to know.

Inside the Sounds office I find that luvable card Mensi of the Angelic Upstarts waiting for me, so I have him sober them up sergeant-major style, and lead the lot of them up to our luxury conference room where eager secretaries made detailed notes of our every word.

They'd signed the usual eight album Virgin deal with a £25K advance for the first one. "We took a lot of things out though," Segs insists. "So we don't have to have coloured vinyl, or 12 inch singles, or a designated producer if we don't want him."

"It'll be most of our established set, all the original numbers from the early RAR gigs till now," adds Malcolm. "We have got a lot of other stuff held back which we're rehearsing as well – obviously there'll be a new set very soon, but the album will be all the familiar stuff, except we're gonna do 'em sooo well..."

Foxy: "Also we're gonna bring some of Misty in for the reggae tracks, Misty's guitarist and their singers. And the punkier tracks, the faster raw tracks, we're gonna do in an eight track studio rather than go in a big studio."

Malc: "Our producer Mick Glossop (Lurkers etc.) is great. He's done really well on 'Babylon's Burning', he knows how to get the best out of us. For example he kept making Paul re-do his guitar bit at the end of 'Society'. First he said 'You trying for a job in Deep Purple?' then 'I think you're a bit of a sap', then 'I think you're a wanky guitarist' and Paul's gone mad. After about eight takes he's so wound up he's wanted to hit Mick and he's done such an aggressive solo... When he came out Mick goes 'I love you'."

Dave: "We'll be producing the album with him, the Ruts and Mick Glossop together."

Malc: "I can see 'Babylon's Burning' in the Top 40, and of course we'll do Top Of The Pops. If you don't do it you must have some sort of hang-up about something..."

"That's all the majority of people see," says Dave. "Where else are they gonna see us?"

ON Radio One last weekend, Malcolm had said that in Southall they used to think a racist was someone who runs fast...

"I've got no big political intentions," he says. "I just voted Labour to keep the Tories out. My lyrics are observational. See, where I come from and where you come from we see the same things and what you see has to come out in your songs."

Foxy: "We don't do the RAR gigs for any political reasons. People who are racialists are blockheads, they just don't think right, and we're just totally opposed to people who think in that stupid way. We're for the right to be a human, to stand against apathy."

Segs: "We do get a few NF skin'eads come to our gigs but Malcolm can handle them, a few at a time. They 'ave a good time dancing to the reggae and go home and think ''ang about...'

"It don't mean nothing to most of them. You see NF demonstrations and the coaches pull up and I swear it's the same people get out every time. They go from town to town. There's only a small number of 'em."

Mensi: "Yeah, but they're a fuckin' dangerous minority."

The room concurs. Let's look at some of the things your songs are observing then. Like the new single.

Malc: "Everyone's singing love songs again so I thought why not go 'BABYLON'S BURNING! You'll burn in the streets! You'll burn in your houses...' It's a short, simple statement and it all leads to one word anxiety. Everyone is anxious. Everyone's worried."

Segs: "It's just an observation; it don't provide any remedies. All we can say is come along to our gigs and enjoy yourself."

I ask about 'Society' and they all burst into song. The words are about state surveillance and 'a media controlled by hate'.

"It's a Big Brother song," says Malcolm. "Every time you get pulled up more goes down about you. They know so much about you..."

Foxy: "And it's gonna get worse now Maggie Thatcher's in. The Tories are in government for five years right? In five years time it's 1984. Five years to build up..."

Segs (out window): "BASSTARDDSS! BASTARRDDSS!"

The Ruts song 'Jah War (Southall)' was written after the anti-Nazi demonstrators' clashes with the police when the NF held an election meeting in Southall last April during which the Special Patrol Group hospitalised Misty's manager Clarence Baker and wrecked the People Unite headquarters. An SPG constable is currently being investigated over the death of anti-Nazi protestor Blair Peach, a Trotskyist teacher from New Zealand.

Malc: "Again, it's observation. I got there that night and wrote down everything I saw. I know a guy died but I didn't know him. But I know Clarence – he got smashed up really bad."

Foxy: "They smashed the People Unite place. 50 of them went in there with truncheons, shields, the lot and they beat up nurses, lawyers anyone who was in there."

Malc: "They had pictures of Clarence and Chrissie – anyone they considered to be leaders – and they went straight for them and beat fuck out of 'em."

Foxy: "There was an Old Bill beating Chrissie, who's a white guy, and Buf, one of our roadies said 'Don't hit him, he's got kidney trouble'. So they turned him over and kicked him in the kidneys. Bastards. They're inhuman. Animals."

Mensi: "Aye, and it's gonna get worse. It's getting to the point where you've just got to make a stand against the bastards."

All: "Yeah, right."

So what's the answer?

"The answer lies in humans," says Foxy. "That's the only answer."

Segs: "I'll tell you what the answer ain't. It ain't the Socialist Workers Party. There ain't a straight political answer..."

Malc: "It's down to humans, individuals."

Foxy: "All we stand for is basic human rights, for everyone, whatever their creed or colour."

AFTER that, as more scrumpy was passed around, the interview degenerated. Talk turned instead to the boys' loud demands to say hello to Phil Lynott, and their plans to launch their own label called Ruttoons if/when they get successful – so they can give bands a break like People Unite gave them. Then Mensi brought up the philosophical paucity of Public Image Limited as he is wont to do, and the band started singing songs your Mum would have found old-hat, like 'Love Letters In The Sand', for fuck's sake, which, knowing that Jess Conrad's 'Cherry Pie' wouldn't be far behind, I took as my cue to skedaddle.

They were in a rut and about to get out of it, out of it....

Mensi apparently later kidnapped one of our messengers and stole her away to South Shields while the scrumpy-blitzed Ruts were put out with the milk bottles by the cleaners in the morning.

And to think they'll be on Top Of The Pops by the end of this month. I ask you, is that any way for pop stars to behave?

Postscript: 'Babylon's Burning' did even better than I'd expected, peaking at Number 7 in the UK chart while the follow-up,

'Something That I Said' (powered by one of Foxy's rockier riffs) got to 29, while the excellent 'Staring At The Rude Boy's managed to reach 22 a year later. The album, The Crack, was bloody marvellous, fusing rock and reggae, punk and protest, in new ways. There's even a jazz-rock feel to the explosive 'Savage Circle'. The cover looked great (particularly as they'd included a rather flattering artist's impression of yours truly at the centre of it), it came with a sticker insisting you 'Don't pay more than £3.99!' and peaked at 16 in the album charts. Not bad for a bunch of semi-politicised piss artists from Southall.

*Malcolm Owen was found dead in a bath on 14th July, 1980. My obituary began: When they pulled his already dead body out of the bath at his Mum and Dad's house last Monday afternoon, there was little doubt in anybody's mind what had killed him. And I'm not going to give you any crap about him dying for a cause, for his art or any of that bullshit. The sad, sick, sordid truth is that he died from a smack overdose. From filthy rotten heroin. If that tragic premature death is gonna have any good effect at all it is to expose once again the hipster-perpetuated myth of the 'wasted' junkie star...and to spell out the plain and simple reality that there is nothing glamorous or heroic or chic about heroin....Smack kills. Full stop.'

HARRY-KARI
Blondie

Newcastle, 1980

I only ever got properly tongue-tied meeting two people. The first was Joe Strummer, the second was Debbie Harry. Read on:

THE woman the tabloids call 'the platinum blonde with the Jean Harlow looks' is perched opposite me on a settee in a Newcastle hotel room. She's wearing a parachute suit, like the one she wears on stage, with white socks and black loafers. Unfortunately she's also wearing a frown like a winter thunder cloud. Debbie has got something on her chest (Careful! – Ed) and it's Britain's gutter press. Leaning forward, she berates Fleet Street's finest and their apparent obsession with her junkie/groupie – or should we say sexually adventurous? – past.

"I think it's irresponsible for the dailies to plug that," she says. "Cos it's encouraging young kids to emulate me. I don't regret the experiences but they're not right for everybody."

I nod in agreement but I'm not taking much in. I'm far too mesmerised for that! Those perfect, angular cheekbones, the full sensual lips, bleached blonde hair, Colgate teeth, dainty nose, and big pale-blue eyes...she is breathtakingly beautiful and cool enough to store a deep-frozen Yeti in. Her skin would look youthful on a woman ten years her junior. But she isn't particularly happy. The more po-faced elements of our music press (i.e. NME) have properly pissed her off.

"These sexism charges are ridiculous," she seethes, looking about as happy as Al Capone with piles. "I like to do what I do and that's why I do it. The most important thing is the audience and they seem to like it too."

I get a feeling this is also aimed at my photographer Virginia Turbett who was bending Chris Stein's ear on the same tedious subject earlier. I try and change the subject and get two word answers. With Virg snapping away and the rest of Blondie watching Ian Dury on the telly I have to admit I ain't exactly pulling a Robin Day out of the bag here. But then perhaps sensing

113

my predicament, Debbie unfreezes; the telly goes off, she shoos the band apart from Chris Stein out to pose for pictures and she smiles at me; a proper, full-on, knee-buckling smile like the sun coming up over the Pacific that lights up the face and defrosts the tension. Either she's taken pity on me or she's decided I'm not out to stitch her up. And we talk. I ask about her chances of reproducing her current UK success back home.

"Blondie's evolution has been natural and organic," she says. "It was never forced. We were just at the right place in the right time with the right product. We are happening in the States now which is great, but it's difficult because of the size obviously." (Those last few words being the ones every young boy dreams of hearing Debbie Harry say).

"The US music establishment is very diverse," she continues. "But I think they're happy to have a group with a fresh identity. It is hard to make a total impact there, and we're still more of a cult thing but it's changing. Bands like the Bee Gees don't deliver any more. They just pose, they have no heart left. I don't feel that way on stage at all. Sometimes I even fall over."

Can you avoid becoming the new establishment?

"I don't think it's possible," she says slowly, adding: "Well there is a way; you can probably do it by being innovative and stylistic, by setting trends, and metamorphosing, y'know? I can see the band doing something different, but I don't think there's anything left in the world for us to do that'd be completely off the wall. Except politics and I don't think anyone would vote for me. Would you vote for me instead of Maggie Thatcher, Garry?"

I say yes, emphatically. The Iron Lady versus the Atomic Woman? No contest!

"Okay," the world's dishiest Democrat laughs deliciously. "I'll run, I'll run!"

Deborah Ann Harry, as the world would find out years later, was born in Miami, Florida, and given up for adoption at the age of just three months – she used to fantasise that she was Marilyn Monroe's unknown child.

Her adoptive parents were Richard and Catherine Harry, a nice liberally-minded couple who ran a gift shop in suburban New

Jersey. But in the mid-sixties, teenage art student Debbie was drawn to the bright lights of the Big Apple embarking on a life that included waitressing, a folk rock band called The Wind In The Willows, nine months as a bunny girl at the Playboy Mansion...and heroin.

1974 was pivotal. It was the year she met Chris Stein and first bleached her hair.

Back track several hours, and from where I'm sitting Stein looks like a chubbier version of campaigning journalist Paul Foot, his tousled hair spilling over the thick black frames of his thick black glasses, matching the thick black greatcoat the crypt-like cold of Newcastle City Hall has forced him to wear for the sound-check.

Down the front someone's had the bright idea of bringing in two huge red Calor gas heaters, but the logical leap involved from installing them to switching them on has obviously proved too much for them and my teeth are making like castanets on the Costa Packet.

Outside about 30 teenagers are huddled round the stage door like flies around a freshly dropped dung heap, defying double pneumonia for a glimpse of Debbie. About one in five school leavers up here are on the dole. A lot of them wander round the big indoor shopping centre in gangs by day, looking bored and demoralised. Many will be here tonight and tomorrow night and Blondie will inject some stylish glamour into the blank generation's sad, drab wasted lives.

At the side of the hall some enterprising girls have found an open window and poke smiling faces and cheap cameras at the stage as Debbie materialises, hidden behind dark glasses, and matching beret, gloves and inky quilted mac.

She seems serious and eager to get things over with. Two stop-start numbers in and the only problem is a niggling buzz. The band play hunt the hum for a few minutes before leaving the aggravation for the roadies to sort out and fighting a path out onto the plush tour bus.

An unshaven Chris comes down to greet us, smiling like he's known us all his life. We shake and start jawing like the clappers devouring idle chitchat and the meaning of life stuff in a magnum two hour session that flits past like five minutes, with breaks just for him to clean up and pose with Debbie and Anti-Pop's bizarre frontman Wavis O'Shave for the local loonie's scrapbook.

Our hotel is at Gosforth Park, sensibly a good five miles from the gig. This is the posh end of the area far from the heavy industry and terraced houses that characterise most of Geordie land. My room is the flashest place I have ever crashed in my life though due to a desperate hunt for pens when Chris arrives it looks like I've just had it turned over by a Mafia hit squad.

Unruffled, he settles down amid the mess on the settee for a proper chinwag. Born 30 years ago to radical Jewish parents and weaned on Leadbelly lullabies, Chris grew up in Brooklyn in an overtly political and irreligious atmosphere. He got his Vietnam call-up just before Woodstock but a slacker physique and experiments with "acid and all that shit" left him labelled 4F and he spent the weekend at Yasgur's farm instead of Bilko's barracks.

A proper beatnik, he wasn't exactly career-motivated and apart from the obligatory European hike and a brief period living in London's Portobello Road in the early 70s just around the corner from Eno who shared his predilection for glitter and extravagant eye make-up. Stein spent his post-school years "fucking around" on the New York music scene.

He met Deborah through an old mate, NY glitter rocker Eric Emerson whose wife sang with Debs in a high-camp, prop-happy girl-trio called the Stilettos. Chris played guitar with them, embarking on a musical and monogamous relationship with everyone's favourite peroxide blonde that's still going strong.

STEIN AND Harry formed a new band after one Stiletto left for porn and the other for prams. They called it Blondie because "Hey Blondie!" is what blokes used to shout at Debbie in the streets. Her looks were always a big part of the band's appeal. In 1976 Debbie was "Punkmate of the month" – stark naked except for a guitar – in Punk magazine. But the band were more than Debbie's looks too.

The Private Stock import album Blondie which followed their excellent import 45 'X Offender' was the vinyl proof of the band's potential backed up with Rainbow and Hammersmith Odeon appearances in '77. Debbie tells me their first English gig was in

Bournemouth, opening for Squeeze. "We were amazed by the crazy reception, but not so amazed by the spitting. I told them, 'Hey, that stuff doesn't go well with my dress' and they stopped..."

Blondie was a classic, stuffed silly with achingly commercial songs, catchy and melodic, with more snap, crackle and pop than the proverbial pantechnicon packed full of Rice Krispies. Writing in Sounds, Jane Suck called it 'necrophilia that didn't hurt'. Chrysalis snapped up the band from the dying Private Stock for a quarter of a million quid that Autumn, and released 'X Offender'/'Rip Her To Shreds' the following October. Criminally it failed to chart; but the February 1978 follow-up, 'Denis' a sprightly gender-bending cover of Neil Levenson's 'Denise' (a 1963 US hit for Randy & The Rainbows) , fared much better and was the first of an unbroken string of hits. Like 'Presence Dear', 'Denis' came from the somewhat less inspiring Plastic Letters album, but as you know it was the follow-up, their third album Parallel Lines that really established the band. It's Blondie's finest achievement to date, a maelstrom of melodies, tunes and catchy lyrics containing no less than four British Top Ten singles, and the biggest selling UK album of 1979. Aussie producer Mike Chapman, of Chinnichap glam rock fame, should take a fair share of the credit.

The follow-up LP Eat To The Beat was relatively disappointing, containing fewer real gems, but by now nothing could stop Deborah's beautiful, photogenic features being adopted by the mass media to such an extent that The Sun for example over Xmas might as well have been a Blondie fan club circular. In Britain Debbie Harry is a superstar. She is punk's Marilyn, a Bardot for the blank generation. But in the States it's been a different story. The band's 'punk' connotations kept them out of the mainstream limelight until last year's disco smash 'Heart Of Glass' (originally conceived as an urban disco-r&b number in 1975) captured the elusive US number one spot, with follow-up 'Dreaming' creaming into the Top 20 too.

Record business resistance to change is being eroded by the promise of mountainous moolah from the likes of the knackered Knack and the clapped-out Cars. 'New Wave' of a kind has become commercially viable Stateside, and with Blondie's legal and managerial problems sorted out at a cost to the band of a cool million dollars, plus the recent move into the movies, and Clem Burke's famous skinny tie theory, it must be odds-on that Deb and the boys will achieve equal status back home in the foreseeable future. But as the band's success grows so does the angry flack from their detractors to the effect that Debbie has sold her integrity for a quick buck, and chosen to become a sex object and is thus reactionary, even "dangerous."

Now personally I don't hold with this at all, not seeing how beholding a beautiful woman is gonna make you go out and rape someone any more than watching The Sweeney is going to make you have a pop at the nearest armed blagger. Besides, no one breathed a word about Ronnie Spector or Diana Ross. Chris agrees.

"I feel that everyone in rock tries to look as good as they can, even the Clash do; it's just an obvious thing. I like taking pin-up shots of Debbie. I like the idea of the rock star as a pin-up. Bowie was. Bowie appealed to people on a sexual level as did the Stones, the Bay City Rollers, even the Sex Pistols. But our success is obviously to do with more than her looks because lots of women have tried to make it on just their looks and failed."

I say it's another double standards that it's okay for Sting to look handsome but not Debbie, but Virginia Turbett claims bizarrely that Debbie presents a "rape me" image, which is "harmful to women" in general. Chris is surprised. "I don't think Debbie has ever presented herself as a woman being abused," he replies thoughtfully. "She has an open sexuality, but I don't think we're selling sex. In fact I think Debbie represents a certain amount of power on stage. She's also showing that women can get to the top."

Evading a cheap women-on-top smirk, I ask how the new wave can avoid duplicating the bad old way of the last establishment.

"I think the most concrete thing you can do is help young artists. I'd like to get a deal like the Specials so we can give bands a start. So far I've produced Casino Music and I hope I can get to do the Lounge Lizards too. We also give free legal advice to young bands which y'know, we wouldn't have got from Keith Richards or anyone like that.

"As for songs with messages I don't think the time is right for us to do them yet. I'd rather save politics for interviews."

How about benefit gigs? The anti-nuclear movement seems big in the States. "I think the anti-nuclear thing is misguided," he says.

"I'm for disarmament, if there were CND gigs I'd play them, but I'm not sure about power plants. If big business is involved it must stink somewhere, but at the same time the first I heard about the anti-nuclear protest there were 10 companies fighting over the record.

"I don't think any one group can change the mechanisms of the industry because to me the music industry is a microcosm of the society as a whole. You're talking about a wider social thing. But I am really excited about the 2-Tone band thing because that is really saying something. It's great seeing black and white kids on stage together. In America blacks have contributed so much to our culture and they're still treated as second class citizens. I hate that racist shit. And over here the battle between Mods and skins and punks is just stupid. It's missing the point that there is a common enemy, the greedy power-mad politicians and the fat bastard businessmen who sap our strength and steal our art."

Does the current jingoistic upsurge around Iran bother you?

"Yeah, but not as much as that Afghanistan shit, that really scares me. I don't think the Soviet system is any better than this one. I think we have to find an alternative to all the old sick systems." Neither Washington nor Moscow, indeed…

The band are on about £100 quid a week per head now, he says. Certainly this tour will lose them money despite being a sell-out. The British baker's dozen and the two Paris dates it consists of are a promo exercise for the new album as well as being a thank you to the Blondie's supporters.

Stein goes out of his way to encourage fans. For Debbie it's harder. Imagine what it'd be like if every time you went out you were as conspicuous as a rhino in the Savoy. In Edinburgh last week she was thumped twice by friendly crowds and so they've had to fly up a bodyguard (a big guy, like Chandler's Moose Malloy, not more than six foot five tall and not wider than a beer truck). But according to Chris it is the press rather than the people who have affected Debs most, people who were as nice as pie to her face to win her confidence and then stitched her up in print.

THE GIG attracts a Jamboree Bag mix of a crowd with all the current youth cults well represented plus a lot of 'straight' couples, some of the girls seemingly trying to exhibit the entire Woolworths cosmetics catalogue in one senses-shattering go. Blondie kick off with 'Dreaming'; the sound is good and clear. It's been said that the band rarely come up to scratch live, but their performance tonight begs to differ. Debbie is the visual mainstay of course, challenged on the eyeball grabbing front only by Clem Burke's exhibition drumming. She is sporting a thin light green jumpsuit and proudly dominates the stage with her hands on her hips and that smile on her lips because she knows that it kills you.

Her sexuality isn't forced or manufactured. It's entirely natural. But what I notice just as much is the power of her pipes. Debbie's vocals range delightfully from the fragile purity of 'Shayla' the factory girl to the wild banshee screaming of 'Victor' the defector.

Sadly the crowd screw up a bit, staying as cold as an Eskimo's out-house for the first half of the set. They only unfreeze when Deb says "I can't believe it, the front row is empty", and the band strike up a medley of old favourites; everyone a bull's-eye.

By the end there is as much chance of them not getting an encore as there is of Mary Whitehouse getting nicked outside for soliciting.

Arriving back at the hotel in a mood not far off the well chuffed I find time working against me again and though I get a chance to chat with Farfisa grinder Jimmy Destri about his plans to work on his pal David Bowie's next album (which would have been Scary Monsters but the collaboration fell through because Destri wouldn't take direction). I don't get time to talk to Clem about Mod and emaciated neckwear, or Stockport's own bass wiz Nigel Harrison about what it's like being 'The English One', or to ask guitarist Frank Infante why he's called 'The Freak' but frankly the view is better where I'm sitting.

How do you keep so trim, Debbie?

"I diet," she says. "I like swimming and skating. Chris works out in bed" – Not like that! Your minds! Well I'm sure he does, and often, but that's not what she means. "He exercises in his sleep," she laughs. "Tossing and turning...he must do a couple of miles every night..."

DEBORAH HARRY was born on Independence Day, 1945, growing up in a middle class home. At high school she was an outsider with a penchant for black clothes and dying her mousey hair in pastel strips. She was an odd mix she says, sensitive on the inside with a tomboy exterior. "Boys scared me when I was younger, but when I reached my teens I was ready for them."

Unleashed in New York she discovered drugs, rock, sex, and danger. In the early 70s she was trying to get across town to a party.

"It was about 2am and I was trying to get a cab, because I was wearing these huge platform shoes and I was struggling.

"This car kept circling and the guy driver was offering me a lift. I said no a few times but eventually because I couldn't hail a cab I took the ride. As soon as I got in, I knew something was wrong. The guy stank so bad I decided to get straight out again only there wasn't a handle on the inside at all. The car had been completely stripped bare.

"Somehow I managed to force the window down and get my arm over to open the door from the outside. He realised and sped up but it actually helped me because I fell out and into the path of an oncoming cab."

Later she recognised the driver on a TV news report. It was Ted Bundy. Yeah, the serial killer.

OUTSIDE OF music, Blondie have taken the almost obligatory step into films proper – as opposed to Deb's past underground movie appearances. There are two flicks scheduled for release this year in the States, the £3 million comedy Roadie starring Meatloaf and Blondie as themselves involved in fight scenes with dwarves (!), and crime mystery movie Union City where Debbie plays a Thirties housewife slowly losing her marbles. Chris Stein wrote the theme music to it, jazzy period stuff, and has expressed an interest in writing more of the same.

I wondered after that and the video disc which the band rate, whether Debbie was into the idea of a multi-media future, and the consequent step closer to the glacial screen goddesses – 'Marilyn and Jean, Jayne, Mae and Marlene' – who she so obviously admires. "I guess so," she says. "But I don't feel I'm in any high pressure situation. As I said the whole Blondie thing has evolved naturally and will continue to. I'm a character, not just another pretty face in line for a part."

Which is the sort of quote you end articles on, except I've forgotten the obligatory Blondie message to Sounds readers: "I'm very happy that we made it back here. I don't think people realised the litigation we've been through and how we've been ripped off and plundered. I'm glad people still like us. The audience still treat us great and that's why we're doing this tour – for the people. And I want all the critics to do their worst and all the fans to love the shows."

I asked for some autographs and went home.

Why the feck I forget to get a picture is anyone's guess. I bumped into Chris and Debbie many times in New York after that and always got on well with them because they were bright and genuine and they knew I wasn't out to stitch them up. Good people.

MODS WITHOUT PARKAS
Secret Affair

Watford, June 1979

'HEY, don't crowd me/I wanna be the only one/Hey, won't you give me a break?/ I'm gonna be second to none...'

LEGS astride, but immaculately trousered, Ian Page punches the air and sings. Yeah, sings. No need to shout when you've got a nifty, nasal whine of a voice as confident and full-throated as this skinny, well-tailored eighteen-year-old.

Page sounds like a reincarnation of minor sixties star Jess Roden, but dresses much better. And his belief in his band and his message burns like the Olympic flame...

The band is Secret Affair, the message is Mod and the medium is a set packed to bursting point with heart-felt, sing-along anthems. Page's lyrics are steeped in ambition, bravado and enough self-belief to over-come the pain of rejection.

'See us roaming these London streets/Feel those last year stares look down on old fashioned feet/Cos we're the Glory Boys — so scared of getting old/Yeah, we're the Glory Boys — we may look cold, but our hearts are gold...'

There are four Glory Boys on stage tonight, but vocalist Page in his sharp two tone teenage blue whistle is the visual mainspring. He's dancing Jack Flash, pills almost audibly rattling round his tin-ribs as he lives through the twelve numbers and then feeds off of the encores this modest but appreciative Watford crowd demand.

This band get encores as naturally as hot Saturday nights grouse and grizzle into grim Sunday mornings, and you don't need to be Bamber Gasgoigne to work out the whys and wherefores of that particular truth.

Like the Specials, Secret Affair are a dance band rooted in sixties music but whereas the Specials are firmly grounded in Bluebeat, the Affair take their base from the glorious early sixties sound of soul, the big wheels of Tamla Motown, the greatest pop catalogue ever written and, like Ska, the original soundtrack to the glorious 1960s Mod subculture. It's music you can dance to which still has a bit of what music experts call bollocks, a slice of aggression served with melody and a bucket-load of commitment.

Contrary to their plans, and almost against their will, Secret Affair find themselves as leading lights in the current Mod Renewal; but they're also much more than that, much broader musically, and many miles from any post-punk connotations. The noted mod fanzine Maximum Speed called them a 'new wave soul band' which hits the nail bang on.

They will also be the first band to transcend the movement.

I say this firstly because as well as being as tight as Tommy Cooper at a pay bar, they also write songs possessed of that sort of instantly memorable irrepressible hook-line that can cause acute embarrassment on the morning after the gig before when you find yourself singing them out loud on the 9.05am Kidbrooke to Charing Cross choo-choo.

SO far, in under five gigging months Secret Affair have built up a solidly loyal street following. They regularly pack out the Marquee and have generated a buzz, spelt BUZZZZZZZZ, so loud round the West End agencies and A&R departments that it all but deafens innocent bystanders and causes great distress to footloose and fancy free flea-bitten mongrels for miles around. How big is this buzz? Imagine a battalion of Brobdingnag bees confined in a giant up-turned jam-jar and then magnify it twenty times. This band is hot.

Yet six months ago most 'informed commentators' would have confined Ian Page and guitarist Dave Cairns to the elephant's graveyard of failed music biz hopefuls, and daubed the word 'Hubris' on their tomb.

The two young men, who craft Secret Affair's songs, were formerly the backbone of the New Hearts, all round flopperoonies who floundered in the power-pop plague and played their last ever gig at Reading Festival last year. They'd signed to CBS in '77 and finally got out of the contract last month (the retainers stopped four months ago, they've lived on savings and intermittent gig income ever since).

The pressures, false promises, phoney friendship and the frustrating hollowness they experienced at the hands of the Biz have made them cynical and bitter. "So," explains Ian. "When we decided to form Secret Affair, we put an advert in the music press small ads: 'Drummer and Bassist wanted —must have a grudge against the business.'"

This attracted Dennis Smith, formerly of Advertising, on bass and Chris Bennett on drums. They spent the second half of last year writing their set and played their debut gig at the Jam's secret Reading University do at the beginning of this year. But the band weren#t entirely happy with Bennett and finally managed to lure Seb Shelton away from the Young Bucks in April to replace him.

Both Dave and Ian are extremely articulate, Ian firing words out like an out of control Gatling gun. Before the gig, in the dressing room with the Purple Hearts, he's completely unmanageable, playing the Coronation Street theme on his trumpet and living out strange delusions of grandeur: "I am a Hamburger", "I am a dressing room" und so weiter. You are unhinged, pal.

"It's worth playing with Secret Affair just to watch Ian going through his tantrums," opines Purple Hearts singer Rob Manton.

True enough, but it's not exactly the best environment for in-depth interviews. So I drag the Hamburger and Dave Cairns out to the car park where in true British barbecue tradition we shelter from the teaming rain in a quiet Volvo backseat and-get down to business...

"WE CHOSE the name, Secret Affair" Ian explains, "because we all had a real no-bullshit attitude to what we were going to do. We weren't going to let anybody get their hooks in to us, y'know? It was the old cliché, if it works or if it falls to pieces we've done it our way. We've done exactly what we've wanted to do with no compromises — we don't need them bastards. If anybody was interested they're quite welcome to come along but then they'd be in on the secret."

East End Mods, many of them ex-skinheads, started getting in on the secret early on. "We really didn't know Mod was going on," Ian is at pains to explain. "Our original idea was to have this group of kids called Glory Boys, a new kind of kid walking up and down Wardour Street taking the place over. And what they were, was kids with suss - they knew about the inside of the music business which made them cynics, but it was because they knew so much that they could be optimistic. That's why they could, change things.

"The original idea was that we'd go out and do so well live that we'd build up a really big following, so we literally had to be signed up — like the Banshees. But the Mod thing crept up on us...It's funny 'cos the New Hearts had always been very strictly a sixties based band, the clothes as well. I used to wear a red suit — that was a big Mod thing — Dave used to wear ties and button-downs, all the band used to wear striped blazers but we never used to say we were Mod because we weren't conscious of that. Us and the Jam were the only two bands at the time who looked smart and interestingly enough when we first toured with them in '77 the papers called it 'The March Of the Mods'.

"When our second single came out one reviewer said, 'This lot sound as if they could be riding Vespas and wearing parkas!'"

Yeah, but you were never that good, were you? I say, playing devil's advocate. That's why so many people are now asking how come this ropey old power-pop outfit has spawned a band like you.

Not for one moment does Dave Cairns look like he might chin me for my cheek. Instead he simply acknowledges the point and says: "It was lack of musicianship in a lot of ways. The ideas we had were like high energy and very sixties but there was no dance beat. Nobody could dance to the New Hearts — it was bad musicianship in the rhythm section. That's why we've got these guys in.

"Our lyrics have changed too — it's just the way we've grown up over the last two years, but a lot of the ideas are the same; the frustrations are still the same."

"Except now we've got more suss," says an animated Ian – 'suss' is one of his favourite words. "We won't get fooled again."

How do you feel about this 'new wave soul' tag you've been given?

"It's okay in terms of old soul," Ian replies. "See if there was a formula to what we do, it would be, like, you listen to any old Tamla Motown track and if you take out the bass and drums and the feel of the bass-and drums, then add an angry powerful guitar and lyrics that apply to today instead of a silly love song then that is us, that is our sound. The bass and drums provide the dance, the guitar provides the energy and the lyrics provide the thought."

Dave goes on: "A guy from Maximum Speed said on London Weekend telly, what's happening isn't just a mod revival, the kids are starting to dress smart and get into music that isn't disco but is danceable — that's what we're about. I hate the Mod tag, I can see it all going sour as the press and the promoters move in, but the thing that will stay alive is that the kids are into dressing up and dancing."

Ian: "We hate the interpretation everyone else puts on mod. Yes we are mod but that's completely different from calling something else punk or heavy rock. Mod is a way of thinking, whatever the year, whatever the situation, whatever the music. It's a different approach to what else is happening at the time. That's what mod did then, that's what we're doing now. We're mods without parkas."

Got it, and thank you for the headline.

HISTORY lesson time. The New Hearts developed out of the pair's earlier college band, Splitz Kidz, who had met at Loughton College in Essex. They were seventeen when they got signed by CBS – two months after their first gig. Kids caught up in a manufactured hype. They were young, naive and understandably pissed off when Powerpop was shot-down by the music press and turned on by the punks. Joe Strummer dismissed the Powerpop bands in 'White Man In Hammersmith Palais': 'You've got Burton suits, ha, you think it's funny, turning rebellion into money...'

The New Hearts never 'got' the politics. They'd seen themselves as being in the mould of the Hot Rods and Dr. Feelgood. Their two singles, '(Just Another) Teenage Anthem' and 'Plain Jane' failed to bother the charts.

Walthamstow-born Cairns, now 20, is the son of an Epping Forest GP who learned the guitar after seeing The Who play Charlton Athletic's ground The Valley (Floyd Road) in 1976. He was sixteen when he formed the New Hearts with Ian Page (real name Paine), who'd grown up listening to his older brother's Motown collection.

"It wasn't a very good band," Ian acknowledges. "But I did learn a lot of things during the New Hearts period. What we were doing was learning the craft of the three-minute pop song."

Their bitterness about the backlash that helped crush their first band translates in the lyrics of 'Time For Action'; a song written entirely by Dave, including the controversial line 'We hate the punk elite'.

"That refers to the tinsel-and-tat merchants," Ian Page explains. "The mob that made punk just another record industry movement and killed the spirit dead. The best thing about punk to me was the message – the idea of breaking away from the industry, but of course for all the anti-establishment talk they didn't actually do it. The Clash signed to CBS, the same as we did."

Is Mod just a handy bandwagon for you?

Ian: "We never refer to ourselves as Mod."

Dave: "What a lot of people are missing is the smartness. People seem to think that being Mod means wearing a parka with a Who sticker, over an old 'Target' t-shirt and looking scruffy. THAT ISN'T MOD. Mod was fashion and the Who came fucking years later. Fashion."

Ian: "And that isn't 'sheep-like', it's the opposite. It's people shouting out for themselves and trying to make themselves as individual as possible — you get a basic idea of what Mod looks like and the whole idea is to look as different from the rest as possible within that framework..."

Dave: "And our kids care about their clothes. If you come to our gigs, the kids are all in smart suits and the only ones who turn up in parkas have got scooters outside. Our kids are into fashion. They go out every week looking for clothes and they're into go-go not pogo and that is what we're about."

Go-go Not Pogo! Another potential headline. These guys are wasting their talent with music, they should be Fleet Street sub-editors.

When the East End Glory Boys latched on to Secret Affair they invited Page down to the Barge Aground in Barking. "I was blown away by it," he recalls. "The place was a sea of suits, and parkas, and good haircuts. It wasn't how I'd envisaged the Glory Boy look. I'd seen it more as spiv-like: suits, black shirts, white ties. But these kids were Glory Boys, they were sharp and they were sussed. And the look they'd chosen for themselves was Mod."

Most of them were working class ex-punks and ex-skinheads who had become disillusioned with the movements they had been part of. Secret Affair flourished on the East London Mod circuit, playing venues like the Bridgehouse in Canning Town. They weren't the only band on the block, but they were the only ones you could dance to – Page's manifesto being to "take the disco out of dance music." And it's working. Their following is growing; the industry that kicked them out is now sniffing around them like a bloodhound on the trail of a killer in Winalot pants.

And if the message still hasn't sunk in, chew on some lyrics:

'Because these days of change will stay, remain/And the need for change don't need a new wave...' (Days Of Change)

'This is my world today/My world you're livin' in everyday/And this is my world today/And I couldn't have it any other way in my world' (My World)

And best of all: 'Standing in the shadows, where the in-crowd meet/We're all dressed up for the evening/We hate the punk elite/So take me to your leader/Because it's time you realised/That this is the time/This is the time for action/Time to be seen...' (Time For Action)

Speaking personally, I'm rather fond of the punk elite, but I won't disagree that this is indeed the time for action, and in the words of another SA song, the time for a new dance. Watch them deliver it.

Watch out boys, your secret life's no secret any more.

INFA...A COME-BACK!
Infa Riot

Genoa, Italy May 2013

VETERAN street-punk band Infa Riot are storming Europe on piece-rate – they're playing one gig in one city a month. So far this year they've blitzed Paris, Zurich, Stockholm, Berlin and on May 3rd, Genoa where I watch the fearsome four-piece blast out an hour of brickwall Oi! to a young and grateful Italian crowd. They're a tight unit, upfront and confident. "We don't hold back or hide behind our instruments," singer Lee Wilson tells me. "We expose ourselves on stage..."

Mercifully I missed that bit. What they do expose is Lee's life-long love of punk rock terrace anthems with huge football chant choruses – all co-written with guitarist Barry Damery. Old Infa favourites like Riot Riot, We Outnumber You, Each Dawn I Die, and of course Five Minute Fashion are better received here than I remember seeing them back in the day...

I haven't caught Infa Riot live since 1981 and I'm struck by how much their gigs have changed. For starters no-one throws a punch all night. The first two shows of theirs I went to were like trailers for Fight Club. In March 1981, the Infas played the Acklam Hall in West London with Millwall skinhead band the Last Resort. The tooled-up LGS (Ladbroke Grove Skins) who supported QPR, besieged the venue looking for West Ham. At one stage they tried to smash their way in through the roof. Ironically, most Hammers Oi fans were in the relative safety of Upton Park at the time, watching their boys battle Dinamo Tbilisi in the Cup Winners' Cup.

"We were headlining that night," Lee recalls. "We played one note of the first song and the LGS started trying to smash their way in. Me and my mate Jasper, who was Spurs, had secured the main doors, so they were getting in through the roof! All I could think of was saving our new drum kit which was Perspex – we'd just bought it off Decca Wade. I'd spoken to a few of them earlier, they said they were after 'all these cunts from East London'. I told 'em we were from Wood Green, North London, which they didn't seem to mind, but I knew there'd be trouble. It was in the air. If the Old Bill hadn't shown up we'd have been properly done."

Lee laughs. "Micky French promoted that gig and we didn't get a penny," he says, his original Plymouth twang creeping into his voice as he considers the thing he holds most dear. Cash. "He said 'Come down my shop, the Last Resort, and I'll weigh you out in t-shirts, which we did, but you know what those shirts were like – one wash and they fell apart..."

Then there was Southgate, the New Punk Convention, which saw West Ham Poplar Boys slug it out with a smaller Arsenal crew led by Upstarts fan Dave Smith, a boxer with one of the fastest jabs I'd seen. "I promoted that one," Lee moans. "I had Ashley Goodall from EMI and Tracy Bennett from Phonogram in for it, so that was our chances of getting signed by a major properly fucked..."

Not that it stopped their debut album, via Secret Records, from charting. We'll draw a discreet veil over the second album...

That first LP was Still Out Of Order, a title which fits tonight's audience pretty neatly. They're mostly skins with the odd Mod and a smattering of leather-clad postcard punks with hair like angry dandelions.

To the eternal horror of the British media, Skinhead was never ever going to be a five minute fashion. But these young Northern Italians would blow their tiny minds. For starters the gig is inside a massive squat. It's run by anarchists, whose black and red flags brighten up the dressing room; the skins and punks are entirely anti-fascist, and there isn't a punch thrown in anger all night.

Punk is heavily politicised across Europe, and the Oi scene here, as in Bologna, leans heavily to the radical left – as exemplified by socialist support band Klasse Kriminale, who are without doubt one of the tightest Oi! bands in mainland Europe.

Street culture matters in this Italian city, once known as "La Superba". I'm here DJing with my Mod oppo, Paul Hallam, and after the sound check the promoters tell us they want to take us all to see "something special". We reckon it'll be something to do with Renaissance art or Columbus, who was born here. Lee is hoping it's a Silvio Burlosconi style Bunga Bunga party.

Instead they take us to a customised Oi! pub serving London Pride on draft. It's decked out with punk and skin memorabilia,

Union Jacks, a West Ham banner and the Cross of St George (he's their patron saint as well as England's.) Free pints and pizzas – Lee could have stayed all night.

The North London based Infas once known as the Upstarts' apprentices, reformed properly in 2011 due to popular demand. They re-recruited old drummer Alex Cardarelli and brought in 26-year-old Ska and scooter fan Liam 'Ozzy' Osborne on bass. Before then Barry hadn't seen Lee, who had been working as a locksmith in Spain, for 18 years. And before that Wilson had a shop in Islington selling fireplaces – some supplied in dubious circumstances by Chas Smash's brother Brendan. Now Lee calls himself an antique dealer, so everyone around him calls him "Lovejoy" or "Love-Oi" or the King of the Round-Dodgers, but that's another story. It certainly explains the presence of pristine white fivers in his wallet. The man makes the proverbial duck's arse seem looser than Buster Bloodvessel's bowels.

Wilson is also known as Daktari because of his safari-style shirts. Well, it is a jungle out there...

The Infas were wrongly accused of being politically 'dodgy' by internet zealots for reasons so tenuous they don't bear repetition. In fact, their history of playing anti-racist gigs stretches back to 1981, and earned Lee a steel-capped Nazi boot in the face at London's 100 Club. Back then he said: "These idiots who come to our gigs and sieg-heil haven't got a clue. If the Nazis were in power do they think they'd be allowed punk rock? Of course they fuckin' wouldn't."

Lee wasn't the first to point out the links between racial tension and sky-high unemployment.

I first wrote about the Infas in November 1980, when Lee was an 18-year kitchen worker, his bassist brother Floyd, 16, was still at school, drummer Gary McInerney, 18, had been sacked that very morning, and Barry, then 16, was playing truant. Inspired by the Angelic Upstarts, they built up a solid North London following in their first nine months. I caught them at the Golden Lion in Camberwell and could see why Mensi loved them enough to write their first ever review. The Infas were like the Upstarts' mirror image only younger and marginally better looking. The age thing mattered back then. As Lee pointed out, Jimmy Pursey was an old man of thirty and even Mensi was 24. The Infas were the same age as their crowd. "It's time to kick out these has-beens," Lee told me in that peculiar West Country-Cockney hybrid accent of his. "It's time for a new generation of bands."

Their name was of course an abbreviation of 'In for a riot' but Lee's lyrics were more about dropping out of school and turning to crime. "We don't go to school, we've given up," he sang in 'Kids Of The 80s'. The Infas were adamant that football and music shouldn't mix, not that it made any difference to the firms. Ironically, more than three decades on, Lee's vision of Oi as "enjoyment" has come to pass.

Since reforming, the Infas have proved themselves across the globe, supplying noisy boisterous fun to streetpunk festivals from TNT in Connecticut to Berlin's Punk & Disorderly. "I love these gigs," Lee enthuses. "Kids half our age know lyrics I wrote 33 years ago. There's no trouble, it's just a blast."

They have a mini US tour this summer, then shoot back to play Rebellion festival in Blackpool. Then they'll crack on with writing a new album. "We're taking our time with it," Lee confides.

"We're making it special. It's been a long time. We want it to be worth the wait."

Infa Riot: coming to your city any month now – but slowly.

OTT IN THE OC
The Mo-dettes

Orange County, October 1980

The Cuckoo's Nest club in Costa Mesa, about fifty miles south of Hollywood, is the largest punk venue in Orange County. It claims to have the world's first mosh pit, and every West Coast band worth its salt would play here, including Black Flag, the Vandals and TSOL. Now read on.

Everything seems fine when we pull up outside. I'm travelling with the all-girl punk pop band the Mo-dettes. Virginia Turbett is taking the snaps, not Halfin, and so the chances of the trip degenerating into a Ross-style gross-out seem minimal. We pull up early for the sound check and breeze into the next door bar, a kind of cowboy joint called Zubies to shoot some pool while Louis, the slaphead US road manager, goes to recce the venue. The locals are down to earth and friendly. Well why not? The band members Kate, Jane, June and Ramona are pretty, as was Virge; while me and their roadie Chris, a young skinhead from East Ham, are clearly no threat. We have a beer and a laugh with the resident denim and leather-clad bar-flies.

Then Louis storms in spitting feathers. The club is trying to charge the band extra for the PA and the sound guy, and he ain't having any of it. He has pulled the gig. The mood changes in a moment. The faces of the friendly locals cloud over. We aren't just two geezers with a gang of stunners in tow, we're a band. A freakin' asshole punk band.

The guys playing pool stop and start to tap their cues across their palms menacingly. The odds aren't good. They are twelve or thirteen fully grown geezers. We are five girls, me, Chris, and a "fucking prick with ears". We head for the door, the whole bar follows. Pool cues are being tapped harder, as hard as our hearts are beating. As we step out two cop cars pull up in the parking lot. Hurrah, we think. The cavalry!

Uh-uh. Glaring at us, the cops leave their vehicles, pull out their night sticks, crouch down and start to drum the ground. Then they begin to chant: "Punk rockers go home!" The crowd join in. "Punk rockers go home!" Huh? The girls look Moddish, me and Chris have crops, and Louis is still a bald prick.

What we don't know is that despite the two buildings being owned by the same guy, and them sharing a car-park, there is an on-going war between the Zubies regulars and the Cuckoo's Nest punters.

We head for the tour bus and are relieved when it starts first time. But the nightmare doesn't stop. We drive off, one of the cop cars drives after us. They trail us for an hour, all the way back to la-la land. We convince ourselves we'll be pulled over and left for dead in a ditch. Those with us with any bottle promptly lose it, along with various pills and small wraps of whizz and Charlie. Legs are vigorously crossed, there is no way we'll be stopping for a roadside slash.

All this for trying to play a gig! Imagine the fuss if we'd knocked them for the beers as well...

Postscript: The Cuckoo's Nest was later targeted by a twelve man police team. The following January one of the punks tried to run down two cops in the parking lot. The city council revoked their live entertainment licence soon after. The Vandals immortalised the hostilities between the two clubs in a song called Urban Struggle.

YESTERDAY HAS GONE
Butlins Festival of the 60's

Barry Island, Wales, October 1983

THE Phyllosan pushers are already doing a roaring trade as we step off the train at Barry Island. Inside the gates of the Butlin's camp, Sanatogen is changing hands for silly money and the chemist's shop sells out of Grecian 2000 by tea time. Any wide-boy with a boot-full of monkey glands to flog would make a mint...

Is this Festival Of The Sixties really what 'swinging' was all about? The sixties meant the Beatles, the Stones, Tamla Motown, Dylan, The Who, The Kinks, The Small Faces, psychedelia, Hendrix, Stax, skinhead reggae and, um, Ken Dodd (ask your mum). Stretch the point and you could throw in Twiggy, Jean Shrimpton and Cathy McGowan as well.

Naturally none of the above named are part of this weekend's 35-band line-up, which should have been a clue that this Festival isn't entirely what it claims to be. Any bona fide sixties purist would blanch at the sight of distinctly seventies artistes like Mud and Mungo Jerry on the bill, not to mention t-shirt stands dedicated to that fifties hound dog Elvis (and yes, he is still losing weight). Why, there isn't even a bust of Harold Wilson in evidence, or a shrine to the Pill.

Historical accuracy clearly might not be on the agenda but wishful thinking most definitely is, as the constant anguished cries of 40-plus housewives struggling to shoehorn eighties figures into their authentic sixties rig-outs testify. We're talking mini-skirts and maxi-thighs.

'Have an affair with a potato', invites one of the fast-food stalls. There are plenty here to choose from. But at least when they go bra-less it pulls the wrinkles out of their faces.

Don't get the idea I'm going in for the fashionable knocking of Butlin's as an institution, though. I love the place. To thousands of kids from my background, Billy Butlin was a visionary. The South African born businessman opened his first camp in Skegness in 1936. It provided affordable holidays (two pounds, five shillings a week back then) for predominantly working class families, with funfairs, swimming pools, bars and regimented entertainment supplied/enforced by the Redcoats, as the camp stewards are famously known.

Some seem tough enough to have seen actual Redcoat service at the Battle of Waterloo. And the men are just as bad.

And okay we may call it 'Butlitz' in honour of the 1940s prisoner-of-war camp Colditz which had slightly laxer security, but the gun turrets are cleverly camouflaged these days, and in truth years of holidaying at Clacton and Bognor have left me with a life-long attachment to this very English institution.

The camps were a popular vacation destination for sixties Mods too – Sounds editor Alan Lewis and a pal were once caught trying to steal the entire contents of a Butlin's chalet. Although why anyone would want those contents – a table, some chairs, a clapped-out kettle and a bed that could have doubled as an instrument of back-breaking torture – beats me like a Soho dominatrix (if I'm lucky).

My companions, punk poet Garry Johnson and prematurely balding Business guitarist Steve Kent are equally enamoured with the institution's low-rent magic. We know that the real top of the bill here won't be the music but the crack. If being trapped on the set of TV's Hi-De-Hi doesn't appeal to your sense of humour you probably haven't got one.

QUITE why the sainted Billy chose to open a camp at Barry Island is a mystery as impenetrable as the writings of Ian Penman, ancient Martian hieroglyphics or a Mother Superior's chuff. Possibly all three. Barren Island would be a more accurate moniker. This godforsaken corner of South Wales possesses as much life as a napalmed cemetery and slightly less charm. The camp was built next to a chemical plant which doubles as the local beauty spot. But it hasn't put anyone off. The management invited holiday-makers to go back in time to 1963 when 'She Loves You' was Number One, and middle-aged ravers have responded in their thousands.

It has cost close on £40,000 to book these bands for the weekend, but with more than three thousand paying customers at fifty notes a noggin, and colossal bar takings (over six grand at just one bar one evening), they aren't losing out. You can be damn sure that one thing that didn't get back to the sixties was the price of booze.

Our first task on arrival is to check out the bars. By judicious planning it is possible to drink legally from 11am until 5am the following morning. And so we do, but only for research purposes of course. Secondly, we form an escape committee. Thirdly we check in for a press conference. The Rock Shop had been turned over for press use. A strikingly attractive mixed race Welsh woman called Gill with a voice like Gladys Pugh gargling double-whipping cream and a stare that could open a clam at sixty paces is cracking the whip over the motley crew of Fleet Street hacks. There is no sign of the NME, but a Melody Maker team are here, along with most of their readership.

Gill hits us with the bad news first: fallen prima donna P.J. Proby, the only genuinely iconic performer on the bill, is refusing to do interviews. Of course he is. He's too busy sitting backstage, twiddling his pony tail, swigging bourbon and weeping into his bag of Butlin's chips, thinking "Has it really come to this?"

Heartbroken, we adjourn to the Gaiety Ballroom where genuine sixties pop buffoon Wayne Fontana is strutting his stuff. Previously plain Glyn Ellis, Manchester-born Wayne and his Mindbenders first hit the charts in 1964 with the imaginatively titled 'Um Um Um Um Um Um' (very so-so-so). A couple of hits later, they were relegated to the desperate r 'n' r revival show circuit. As tonight's performance proves, they were shows to miss.

With the guitar lost in the mix and more bass than a Male Voice Choir, the 'Benders work through a stunningly stultifying sing-along-a-K-Tel embarrassment of an act. At least they're consistent: 'Lady Madonna', 'Da Doo Ron Ron'... no matter who wrote it, they ruin it.

Their set has more low spots than a midget's scrotum. It is pure cloth cap cabaret with less finesse than a bin-man's belch. Yet the assembled senile delinquents react with wild applause, which says more about the talents of Mr. Johnny Walker than Mr Wayne Fontana.

Much more entertaining is the solo rendition of 'Banner Man' by a large barmaid who looks and sounds like Janet Street-Porter on steroids; that Street-Porter herself looks and walks exactly like Muffin the Mule gives you an insight into the terrible nightmarish impact of her performance. If we'd been on acid instead of speed, the effect could have been literally mind-bending.

THE evening bill kicks off with Mungo Jerry whose first hit came, appropriately enough, in 1970. They open their set with a fifteen minute sound check behind the dusty black stage curtains in the Pig & Whistle. Then the curtains open and it's downhill all the way. Cheery Ray Dorset introduces a dreary knees-up with a wave of harmonica feedback. I am immediately struck by his resemblance to a slimmer, but even more frightening version of Agony Aunt Claire Rayner; and believe me he needs her advice, he really does have problems. A one point he stops stamping and shouting and starts skipping as if auditioning for the part of "Deranged Extra" in a low-key am-dram production of One Flew Over The Cuckoo's Nest. Very odd.

'Long-Legged Woman Dressed In Black' reveals our erstwhile skifflers in their true light – Status Quo as played by Benny Hill (but nowhere near as good as that sounds). Things pick up with the big hits – 'Lady Rose', 'In The Summertime', 'Mighty Man' and that well-known hymn to the infant branch of EXIT, 'Baby Jump'. Admittedly Dorset does possess a fair pair of pipes, but the Mungos are no better than your average pub combo. Yet again their dated mix of boogie, blues, folk and skiffle goes down well with the undemanding crowd. These people are so desperate for entertainment they'd give a jukebox a standing ovation.

NEXT up is the Mini-Skirt Competition. One woman looks like Munch's Scream dressed by Twiggy and appears to have legs drawn by L.S. Lowry. Her friend is carrying a card with the number 23 written on it. It isn't entirely clear whether this is referring to her contestant number or her weight in stones. When she does a twirl to reveal she is wearing no under garments, bolder blokes than us would also have bolted... back to the Gaiety where we are gutted to learn that we'd missed that other borderline flasher Proby.

Why had a performer of his status gone on so early? Johnson reckons he's had to leave early, to collect his pension...

The legendary trouser-splitter was of course once a genuine superstar whose mesmeric stage act was counter-balanced by off-stage paranoia, self-destruction and self-obsession. PJ, possibly short for Poor Judgement, went bankrupt in 1968, and graduated to lame stage musicals (the dire Catch My Fire and Elvis The Musical, a rotten cash-in which opened in the West End while the King's corpse was still warm) and bad retro TV shows like Unforgettable, which had rightly been dubbed Unforgivable. Such a shame. A genius showman brought low by his own hands. As his dresser must have often said, "That's torn it."

Marty Wilde made up for missing Proby…almost. Born plain Reg Smith in the cradle of culture that is Blackheath, South East London, Marty was once considered quite a sex symbol – stop giggling at the back – and had four big hits…in the late fifties. Sporting more shocking flares than a pyromaniacs' convention fireworks display, Mart and his merry men breeze through a faultlessly professional set of cabaret rock and pop, including a heartfelt version of 'Teenager In Love.' Marty Wilde is 97.

Moaning only about the absence of his far more talented and alluring daughter Kim, we stagger back to the Pig (the pub, not the mini-skirt contestant) which is packed. When I find myself singing along to Edison Lighthouse (first and only hit, 1970) I realise my critical facilities are shot. I bin my Bic and take refuge in serious drinking.

IN the morning I am awoken at 7am by the sound of John Denver piped over the Tannoy system – the evil bastards! Steve Kent revives Garry Johnson with a pint of water – in the face – and we stumble back again to the Pig where an unknown female crooner with all the sensual promise of a heap of compost is destroying 10CC's 'I'm Mandy, Fly Me' (circa 1976). She sounds like she gargles with Ajax.

Over in the Gaiety, the odds-on favourite to be the band of the weekend are about to go on stage: Les Gray's Mud! Yeah, glam rockers Mud, the Chinnichap wunderkinds whose first hit had come in, uh, 1973. They start well with 'Dyna-Mite', 'Tiger Feet', and 'The Cat Crept In', a real retro joy; which is more than could be said for the band's unconvincing Showaddy-shoddy drapes and creepers. Tears stream from my hung-over eyes as Mud power (okay, cruise) through such shameless pop gems as 'Secrets That You Keep' and 'Lonely This Christmas' (Number One in 1974, and more kitsch than Eartha Kitt), but when singer Les introduces 'Y Viva Espana' the magic vanishes like Infa Riot's Lee Wilson at a pay bar.

Gray then trumps this abomination by leading chants of "Oggy-oggy-oggy, oi-oi-oi" in what seems to us to be a transparent attempt to jump on to the South Wales skinhead bandwagon. We're gutted.

A passing punkette called Tiffany (because, she says, she was conceived in a Mecca ballroom) offers the considered opinion that Mud's set is "crap". You have no reason to believe she lied. When they lurch into a rotten rendition of the Smokey Robinson classic 'The Tracks Of My Tears' with all the grace of a deranged clown with a death wish let loose in the fine china department of Sotheby's, Les Gray's name became worse than Mud. Not even the inevitable 'Tiger Feet' could redeem them now.

At 4pm, former chart-toppers Mud carry their own gear out of the venue.

Incredibly they aren't the day's biggest disappointment. That honour falls to Screaming Lord Sutch. His Lordship is one of those people deemed 'legendary' because he's been around for longer than rationing. His career spans three decades and he's not had a hit in a single one of them. Off-stage, Lord Sutch (real name Dave) is about as wild as a sedated dormouse. His set builds to a climax where he lights a small fire on stage but sadly failed to throw his hat on it. Few are impressed.

Sutch's performance is roughly as explosive as a Bagpuss sub-plot. It has more covers than a cruise ship laundry room and as for the "horror" element the sound of Cilla Black gargling backstage before her set in a locked theatre would be a damn sight more threatening.

At his best, Sutch would make a passable stand-in for Max Wall in a theatre matinee with the house lights dimmed.

SUNDAY night offered even fewer musical highlights, but we do find Mond from the Angelic Upstarts in the crowd claiming to be

Joe Brown's roadie. And I take part in an Elvis Presley impersonation contest – imagine the Gonads crucifying 'The Wonder Of You' and you'll get the complete picture.

I come eighth, out of seven; behind a Somalian. Nice woman.

We chum up with a huge Welsh Oi fan security man called Oggy, who we award Sounds 'hero of the weekend' status for refusing to let Emperor Rosko into Buzby's disco without a pass (even though he's DJing there). But from there it's all downhill. We have to make our own amusement on Monday, which mostly involved Johnson tormenting the balding Steve by getting announcements read over the Tannoy system: 'Lost, one gent's wig; if found please return to Mr Kent in chalet number sixteen.' The other wind-ups, which are not even vaguely printable, involved 'love letters' to Gill allegedly from me but actually penned by Johnson, the plum, claiming that she could be Gladys to my Jeffrey Fairbrother and including a sub Hi-de-Hi! invitation to have "wheeze in the pool." Ho-de-bloody-ho.

Elsewhere, jazz leg-end Acker Bilk (born Bernard) proves a hit in the Pig, largely thanks to a wild outbreak of audience 'air clarinet' playing. Billy J. Kramer should have been there watching him. Or rather he should have been anywhere apart from on-stage at the Gaiety.

Billy, born Bill Ashton, was a genuine Merseybeat star notching up six hits in the 1960s (gasp) under the management of Brian Epstein. Four of the six songs were Beatles covers.

Like all the Merseybeat stars, Bill and his Dakotas had a few quick hits and then melted like snowmen in the Sahara. In common with most of the bands here, his set consists largely of r 'n' r standards performed with very little verve or imagination. We calculate that 'C'mon Everybody' is played 39 times this weekend. Sid Vicious could sing it better than Billy...from the grave.

Band of the day, from a purely professional point of view, are Marmalade. Once known as The Gaylords (insert your own puerile aside here), Marmalade never spread themselves too thin, performing a tight procession of hits such as 'Ob-La-Di, Ob-La-Da' (another Beatles song), 'Butterfly' and 'My Little One' (possibly a tribute to Halfin). 'Reflections Of My Life' was and remains the golden shred of Marmalade's set.

Helen Shapiro is a true pro. She doesn't even blink when her version of 'Getting Better' (yep, Beatles again) is ruthlessly sabotaged by radio interference from passing mini cabs picked up on the amps: 'I've got to admit it's getting better'... 'P.O.B. over'... 'A little better all the time'... 'Clearing ten minutes'... 'Can't get no worse'... 'Roger that.' (Definitely, 15 years ago). It's just a shame she wasn't singing 'Drive My Car'.

With a voice as big as Robin Hood's heart, East London-born Helen easily out-classes Clodagh Rodgers, a walking tribute to the embalmer's art whose set is as dull as an over-used simile. Surely only Clodagh's striking resemblance to ET keeps the crowd's interest? Her cheek bones are so high it looks like she really has had a 'Jack In The Box.'

With a name that sounds like a promise, and pins hot enough for her to win today's Glamorous Granny contest, Clodagh can still turn the head of many a would-be geriatric Romeo. It could well be that in the fullness of time her off-spring will evolve into an entirely new sub-species of humanity. Governments will then pass laws to stop them from singing in public.

FINALLY, we are found propping up the bar in the Pig for the last two acts of the weekend. And what better way to round off a Festival Of The Sixties than with two 1950s skiffle acts: Lonnie Donegan and Chas McDevitt? Yeah, you must remember Chas. He had a big hit in 1957 about five years before you were born and could probably make money now by passing himself off as Kenny Rogers. Or a large piece of teak.

Lonnie was of course a household name back in the day. And what a rotten day that was. It's a little known fact that as a three year old in beautiful downtown Charlton, my first public performance was a Lonnie Donegan impression. And going by the Elvis impersonation, let's hope it remains little known.

Lonnie, aw, Lonnie. After 38 pints of wallop how could he be anything less than magic? It is nineteen minutes past midnight when he comes on stage and there isn't anyone in the Pig who isn't seeing double. Including Lonnie. All the hits, including some that should have been misses, cascade from banjo-botherer's lips: 'Rock Island Line', 'Cumberland Gap', 'Puttin' On The Style',

'Wabash Cannonball', 'Gamblin' Man', 'Pick A Bale Of Cotton'...you name a US folk song, he's nicked it.

Lonnie's been playing skiffle for thirty-two years. It doesn't seem a day over fifty-seven...

I wonder if his chewing gum's lost its flavour yet. Or if his old man really is a dustman. Or if he's ever changed his socks. There was a peculiar hum around the Pig that night which we put down to Johnson's many personal problems at the time.

Sadly we are forced to leave Butlin's the next morning, with a string of unresolved mysteries. Like, was it really true about Tiffany's Mum and Lord Sutch, and if so which one screamed the loudest? Why was Steve Kent nicknamed 'The Dog Catcher'? And why did Garry Johnson and skinhead man-mountain Oggy ruin Mr Kent's love-life by sitting on his bed all night? These are the questions. We're not sure we know the answers, but we're going back next year to try and find out...

Postscript: Sadly we never did go back to Barry Island, as Butlin's went understandably "Garrity" when they read this piece and banned me from the camp to salve the hurt they felt over my "cavalier" attitude to their Great Event. It closed in 1996 and is now a housing development.

Lord Sutch stood for parliament for the Monster Raving Loony Party gaining 208 votes, which although unimpressive, was still more than the paying customers he'd attract anywhere in the world. The poor old sod hanged himself in 1999.

Lonnie Donegan died in 2002. Wayne Fontana was jailed in 2007 for setting fire to a bailiff's car. In 2012 PJ Proby was cleared of nine counts of benefit fraud totalling £47,000. And Marmalade play on, albeit with no original members.

Tiffany and her Mohican punkette pal Parrot-head stayed in touch for a while and briefly became backing singers with the glorious Gonads. Steve Kent's hair never did grow back.

SWEET DREAMS AREN'T MADE OF THIS
Eurythmics

Covent Garden, 1987

ANNIE Lennox was no fan of the press, be it rock or tabloid. So it was no great surprise when, to extract a revenge for various imagined slights, Annie invited me to fight the Daily Mirrror's gossip columnist John Blake, properly, in a boxing ring, at the Eurythmics' end of tour party in London's Covent Garden.

If truth be told I rather fancied my chances. Blake, known to his friends as Flakey Blakey, was by his own admission generally regarded as being as slippery as a snake in a sink full of sump oil. He didn't look like he could go two rounds with Olive Oyl. But I still took the challenge seriously. I called up my old pals from the Bridgehouse, Canning Town, for guidance. Glen Murphy best known for his starring role in TV's London's Burning and his dad Terry, who were both great boxers in their time, agreed to train me for the bout at a gym in East London and I was as ready for it as I'd ever be. Which was more than I can say for Snaky Blakey....

The first clue that things weren't going to go to plan came when I was in the ring waiting to go and I spotted Blake was still wearing a tuxedo. He was also wearing an enigmatic smile. Then the music from the Rocky film started to blare out and my hooded opponent entered through the crowd, flanked by two of the biggest minders that you'd ever seen outside of the Long Good Friday. Even then I didn't panic because I'd seen Frank Bruno there earlier and I assumed that it would be him. I knew Frank pretty well and I knew that when he got in the ring we'd have a laugh. Except the figure who climbed through the ropes wasn't as tall as Frank or as wide as Frank. He took off his hood and grimaced in my direction. It was Lloyd Honeyghan, the welterweight champion of the world ...who I happened to know was just weeks away from a title fight against Johnny Bumphus. He looked as happy as a shark with toothache.

My legs started to wobble, but Glen was in my corner and he urged me on: "Go on Gal it'll be all right..."

Well I threw a left and a right, an uppercut, I was dazzling...until the bell rang for the start of round one and Lloyd joined in...

I moved forward, jabbing with my left. A red mist descended over Honeyghan's eyes and he went for me. Blam, blam, blam. He threw a right to my face followed by two vicious left hooks that connected with my chest and collar bone. I hit the canvas like a sack of spuds.

I did have him worried though. For a moment he thought he'd killed me.

The bell went for the end of round one and I staggered back to my corner. "Right," said Glen, "this time, when you get in there, move more, duck and dive and..."

I cannot repeat my reply, ladies and gentlemen, in respectable company. Let's just say I questioned his sanity.

"Gal," he said. "Do it. You'll be fine. Trust me."

So I got back in the ring, uttering private prayers to the Great Architect, and to my pleasant surprise Lloyd was a changed Ragamuffin man, a real honey in fact. He actually pretended my punches were hurting.

Glen had known that his worried corner would have reminded Lloyd between rounds that he was fighting an amateur and he would lose his licence if he didn't ease up.

As the bell rang to end the bout Annie Lennox and Dave Stewart entered the ring and declared me the winner, apologising profusely. I got a £100 cash prize and Help The Aged got a cheque for £5K. But that wasn't the end of the story. The papers went nuts and The Sun ran the report over the whole of Page 5 under the headline 'Chump Champ' with two pictures – one of me on the canvas ('Down but not out...Bushell hits the deck') and one more flattering shot from the second round ('Take that...Honeyghan ducks as Bushell prepares to lay one on him').

All of the papers took the line spread by Lloyd and his manager Mickey Duff that he'd lost his temper because I'd tried to knock him out. Lloyd told reporters that I'd hit him on the chin "and no-one gets away with that." It was absolute nonsense, flattering nonsense, but nonsense all the same. I'd gone in, jabbing and moving, fully believing it was going to be a fun charity bout. But they had to protect Lloyd's licence and it didn't do me any harm to be known as the nutter who had tried to KO the world champ. My quote in the papers was "Bring on Tyson!"

It wasn't the hardest fight I ever had to be honest. That was the divorce in 1999. At least Lloyd didn't take my house. Or my son. But I had several pints bought for me on the strength of it.

I met up with Lloyd not so long ago at an ITV show. He's about three times his fighting weight now and has taken to wearing a Fat Pat style fur coat. I reminded him about our bout and he said he'd gone for me because he'd thought I was a big bloke like Lennox Lewis and might punch like Lennox too. And I was quite flattered by that until I remembered Lennox Lewis wasn't even heard of back then.

I would fight Lennox now though. Annie Lennox. Anything to stop her squawking.

Mind you, these days she'd probably beat me.

THE LARS GANG IN TOWN
Rancid

Chislehurst, Kent November, 2014

LARS Frederiksen was 15 years old when a kid pulled a gun on him in a back alley.

For a second, time seemed to freeze. The other boy, also 15, aimed the weapon straight at Lars's head and squeezed the trigger. By some punk rock miracle, the hand-gun jammed. "He shot, but it didn't go off," Lars recalls. "I was at school with him. He didn't like me because I beat the shit out of him once..."

Frederiksen's life reads like a soap opera. His Italian American father, a brilliant alcoholic, walked out on him and his older brother Robert when Lars was two, leaving his Mum to raise them both in the mean old backstreets of Campbell, California. At eleven, the future Rancid guitarist was banged up in Juvenile Hall, the US equivalent of borstal. He was drunk when the cops arrested him.

"I was charged with cruelty to animals, possession of PCP, breaking and entering," he says. "But I'm not someone who likes to hurt animals for the sake of it. As we were burgling the house, the owner's dog wouldn't stop barking so I wrapped lime green chewing gum around its snout and it got stuck in its fur..."

PCP, for the uninitiated is the street name for Phencyclidine, or Angel Dust. "It's an elephant tranquilliser, it makes you slow. It became known as Angel Dust because the Hell's Angels used it, a lot."

The bikers ran his part of town. "The local politicians changed the name of my street, Jean Drive, because it had such a bad reputation. They brought in a law saying that bikes couldn't be parked in the road but the Angels just gave us ice cream to sit on their Harleys so they weren't technically parked..."

The notorious one-percenters treated his mum with respect, though. She was a Danish immigrant and as tough as old boots.

"My mum grew up in Nazi-occupied Denmark," Lars recalls. "She saw her family dragged out and shot...

"People used to call her the Danish Napoleon, because she was four foot nothing and fearless."

For his first stay in Juvenile Hall, Lars found himself locked up with a 17-year-old room-mate "who'd burned down his house with his father in it…but I wasn't worried in there because it was a lot more violent outside on the streets.

"Inside, we never hated each other because of colour, we were all fucking poor; we were all the same. It wasn't cliqued up like prison movies."

Lars, who just toured Europe with his other band The Old Firm Casuals, got off lightly that first time because his victim didn't want to press charges. But it wasn't to be his only visit.

"I got beaten up by an older kid because he said I was a freak for being into punk rock," he recalls. "And even though he'd attacked me, I had an official warning from my probation officer about it…"

Which meant that the next time he got in trouble, for the minor jape of filling a condom with water and throwing into the girls room, he got sent to Juvenile Hall again…a waste, both of the condom and his time.

THE first time I met Lars, thirteen years ago, he told me that if it hadn't been for Oi! and Sounds he would never have made it through his delinquent teens. Now 43, Frederiksen says "You kept me alive. You gave me something I could relate to utterly.

"When I got out of Juvenile Hall the first time, I'd stolen 20 dollars and I used it to buy Strength Through Oi, that was my shit. You could just feel that these kids were the same of us – the skins, the punks, they were working class like we were.

"Before that we listened to Kiss, AC/DC, Cheap Trick. But they didn't relate to us like the Cockney Rejects and the Last Resort did."

His brother Robert was a skinhead before him and brought home all the good stuff, from Trojan reggae to the UK Subs via the Oi compilations and imported copies of Sounds which were sold in Tower Records.

Lars wore his dad's Sta-prest (action slacks). "We were looking on the back of your fucking Oi albums trying to figure out how to dress!" he laughs. A picture of Lars aged eleven duplicating Micky

Geggus's v-sign gesture on the front of Oi! The Album can be seen on the OFC's tasty 'Born Criminal' single.

He inherited a life-long love of skinhead reggae from the UK scene too. "I got some stick for citing Oi as an influence," he says. "But I thought Oi music was saying we're all the same, punks and skins – that skunk rock thing."

He pauses and adds "I didn't know what a fucking 'Herbert' was though." It was just another way of saying a terrace tearaway at the time; they were prototype Casuals. And of course Lars loves football too. He's Millwall through and through, with the club's Lion emblem painted on his guitar. "Blame that on Roi," he laughs, referencing Last Resort singer Roi Pearce. "Steve Whale and Micky Fitz from the Business took me down to West Ham, my brother was a West Ham guy. But I felt more at home at Millwall." He had his first tattoo when he was eleven, too. "I got Oi! on my shin. But as I grew up it moved to my ankle. Mum was so pissed…" He currently sports more tatts than the seventh fleet, far too many to count. Lars loves ink so much he has become a tattooist himself. Four years ago he opened his own tattoo parlour in Tokyo which he co-owns with Tokyo Hiro and Shaw Tanaka. It's called Skunx, the old term for skinhead and punk unity which is also inked on his forehead.

LARS'S life of crime ran parallel to his growing love of music. At 16, he and his mates broke into a house high on speed, and found a dead guy in there. He'd been there for a while. "We'd climbed through kitchen window and saw an old man in a chair. He looked like he was asleep, but it smelt really bad. We did the responsible thing, we nicked the twelve pack of beer out of his fridge, and called the fire department. Then we sat opposite and watched the chaos drinking the beer, we were such arseholes!"

He is completely teetotal now. "When I drank I had an allergic reaction," he grins. "I broke out in handcuffs…"

Speed didn't do it for him, though. "I was never into crank, I was always a downer guy. I wanted booze. On speed I'd just stay up masturbating all night. You're rubbing it raw, Garry."

Sounds like you were…Apart from reading imported copies of Sounds as a kid, he was hooked on DC and Marvel comics. But

English punk was his real love. "I liked Social Distortion but a lot of what I listened to was English - the Business, Discharge. I always felt my Mum's Danish drinking songs were a bit like Oi, they had the foot-stomping, the mob choruses, the beer..."

At the end of the 1980s, Lars joined the UK Subs. "We been playing an all-day punk festival and I met Charlie at bar. My band had done a cover of 'Organised Crime' and he liked it. We had a few drinks, he said they were losing their guitarist Karl Morris, I said 'I'll do it...'"

Tim Armstrong, formerly of Operation Ivy, asked Lars to join Rancid when he was 21 and the band proceeded to write their own unique and still flourishing chapter of punk rock history, using their influences – essentially the Ramones, 2-Tone and Oi to create something of their own. "Working class music," he says simply. "My choice as a kid was – join army, lot of my friends did and they died, or continue to rob and steal. All I really wanted to do was play music, and that's what I've done."

Not everyone was thrilled when Rancid's independently released And Out Come The Wolves album went platinum.

"People accuse us of selling out because we've sold a million records, but punk is cool - that's why it got popular. All the rest was shit, hair metal, 'look at me and my Corvette and my blonde big-titted girlfriend' that wasn't for me.

"Punk now is about making a life for yourself, a better life, it's about thinking for yourself."

Politics is always a contentious area, both in punk and street-punk. A lot of US punk seems to be either hippy-green or libertarian.

"I'm right down the middle, I believe in the death penalty as much as I believe in a woman's right to choose. You have to be able to make up your own mind. It's annoying when I see people sucked into politics when they know nothing about it. Most of the problems in the world stem from politicians, not what colour your skin is or your religion. But I'm not pro the religious right, they have their own political agenda."

Lars is forceful in his opinions, but not over-bearing. His intention is to be understood. Even now you still meet snobs or ignorant people who think that all skins were/are racist. "The PC motherfuckers in Germany don't like us. But being patriotic is not fascism. I love where I come from, and I love my Danish roots. And by the way, Number 1 you're German…you invented that shit.

"I've been called a fascist, and I've been called a Communist. I'm not either!! I have my own beliefs. If you're a child molester you should have your dick cut off…"

TRAGEDY touched Lars's own life in 2002 when his brother died from an enlarged heart.

"For the last few weeks of his life we were getting along. He called the night before he died, and I was off doing interviews for Rancid, and left a message saying 'Hey, I just wanted let you know I had a really good time with you. I just wanted you to know I love you.' And I'd give anything now to tell him how much I loved him too."

Lars feels differently about his own father now than he once did.

"He grew up in Juvenile Hall, his mum gave him away at four. Then he was in a foster care home. He was never there for us; he was an alcoholic. But now I have a lot of forgiveness for him."

Lars rates umpteen modern street-punk bands including Bishops Green, Duffy's Cut, Assault & Battery, Victory, NOi!se and Argy Bargy. "That last album raised the bar. Whoo! I didn't know that Watford Jon, from Luton, albeit a cunt, could sing like that!"

He has punk loads back into the scene, producing bands and creating the Hooligan classics series of seven inch eps that functions like the old Oi comps.

"The great thing about original Oi was that nobody sounded the same. To me Oi was everything rolled into one…and I still can't play Mick Geggus's guitar solos!

"My message to anyone reading this is: start a band. Everybody's a fucking critic, don't listen to them, listen to your heart and do what's necessary, whatever the consequences."

This Means War is the OFC's first real full-length album. In it, Frederiksen takes his life-long love of streetpunk, all those great brickwall influences, and builds on them, re-energising the sound and as a byproduct the scene itself.

Rancid have also just released a new album, Honor Is All We Know, which to these ears sounds like their best work since And Out Come The Wolves. But Lars insists "My kids and my wife are the most important things to me. I get up in the morning, I have a coffee, take a shit and take the kids to school. That's what I do."

He is married to second wife Stephanie, a yoga teacher "but not a fucking hippie." They have two sons, Wolfgang, seven, and Soren, who has just turned three. "I'm a regular person. I'm not some cool guy. I'm a dumb kid with a terrible education who got lucky.

"I'm not a millionaire, contrary to popular belief. Punk and Oi, that's my culture. That's what I am, that's what I'm going to be! I don't look for people's acceptance. I'm going to be there if you like it or not.

"My life was tough. We were working poor before it was a fucking term, I've got the sob stories. And when you come from an area like that no matter how far you climb you'll always be working class. And you know what? I don't give a damn cos I'm proud of what I am."

BONANZA BEANO
Max Splodge

Waco Texas, June 1981

OH great. It's 9am. I've been up all night with Motörhead and now some no-good dirty bastard is ringing my hotel room. The call is collect, the voice familiar. "I 'eard you was over," croaks a cheery South Londoner. "Fancy popping dahn to my little 'ouse on the prairie?"

Max? Max Splodge, is that you? "Yer," the voice replied. "I'm in Texas." "Why?"

Max tells me Splodgnessabounds have played a handful of unadvertised gigs in the Deep South as part of their new 'Cow Punk' initiative. He says he's stayed over and rented a luxury ranch house, and that I should come down "for a top exclusive."

Thirty hours later I'm standing in front of the sort of place you might conceivably describe as 'luxury' but only if you'd been raised by wolves and were unfamiliar with the concept of roofing. To call it a shit-hole would be to insult shit-holes. It would need doing up before it could be condemned. The windows are shattered. Patches of paintwork curl up at the edges. The woodwork looks like it's survived a seven generation plague of woodworm. Either that or Max has been playing ball against it with hedgehogs.

"Whadya reckon Gal?" asks Max, beaming proudly. "I bought it with the royalties from 'Bicycle Seat'." (Later I find that the hovel actually belongs to the seedy promoter who sponsored Splodge's secret dates.) Nice, I say. Where's the band?

"Gone 'ome, mate," Max grunts. "There's only Smacked Arse O'Reardon left. It got a bit 'eavy." And so has Max. The gut on him! Either he's got his own brewery out here, or he's six months pregnant. With twins. I notice a mob of blokes hanging about like cattle-hands waiting for a herd. Sporting mirror shades and chewing matchsticks, they look like a badly dressed Clint Eastwood Convention. The t-shirts and jeans are punk; but the boots are snakeskin and the hats, like Max's beer belly, are ten gallon. Who are these in-bred retards? I ask pleasantly.

"They're the cow punks," says Smacked Arse, also known as Willy Strang. "They're who inspired our latest e.p."

Ah yes, 'Cowpunk Medlum'. Released by the time you read this, the title track is a moving mix of spaghetti Western and a punked-up retread of 'Do Not Forsake Me, Oh My Darling.' It's less High Noon, more High Wycombe. "Cow Punk is the future," Max gibbers excitedly. "It's the next wave. Sort of Cunts & Western. It's the latest thing round here."

Of course it is. Right on cue, Splodge manager Brian Bonklonk materializes with a generous mug of sipping whiskey which he thrusts into my grateful mitts. "Cow Punk is like Oi! but in the States," Bonklonk purrs. "Cow Punks here are taking on rednecks like we're taking on straights back home."

Splodge aren't exactly going down here like a fat bloke in quicksand here. "We had a lot of opposition at gigs," admits Max, nicking my whiskey and sinking it in one. "Tony Day" – Splodge's rhythm guitarist AKA Tone, Tone the Garden Gnome – "got his arm broken at the last gig we played. It was like a big bar-room brawl in a cowboy film. It was lucky no-one got seriously hurt. That's why the band fucked off. Wimps! Rednecks even invaded the ranch and tried to set it alight. We had to fire off a few shots, I can tell you."

One of the joys of interviewing the Artful Splodger is the challenge of sorting out the facts from the fiction. He does love embroidering the truth with, shall we say, a generous smattering of whimsy. But that's what happens when you deal with Pathetique bands; reality plays second fiddle to invention and only the dullest of interviewers would insist on stopping the great nitwit in full flow. Like all genuinely funny people, Max creates his own comedy universe. He's going where the likes of the Goons and Rambling Syd Rumpo have gone before, only with coarser songs, more alcohol and a greater reliance on breaking wind.

Splodgnessabounds originally formed over a cab office in Peckham, South London, winning a recording contract with Deram the old-fashioned way by coming second in the 1979 Battle Of The Bands contest. Their first hit was an accident. 'Two Pints Of Lager & A Packet Of Crisps' was the un-promoted under-belly of their debut single 'Simon Templar'. It peaked at Number 7 in the UK charts a year ago. The follow-up ep, a jaunty cover of Rolf Harris's 'Two Little Boys', managed to reach 26 in the charts. (The two other tracks, the unpleasant 'Butterfly Song' and 'Horse' were closer to capturing Max's madness. 'Horse', or rather 'Saying Goodbye To His Horse' was a ditty his grandad used to sing to him; it was adopted by Splodge's Charlton Athletic hooligan following to the extent that it became a Charlton terrace anthem...even though Max is Millwall. This year's self-titled debut album was packed with comic nonsense such as 'Porky Scratchings' and tear-jerking tales like 'I Fell In Love With A Female Plumber From Harlesden NW10'. It flopped like a sack of spuds, but hey ho, there's no accounting for taste.

Chaos has followed Splodge since the start. Live shows witnessed frequent public nudity and sphincter-straining flatulence, cuing outrage and police intervention. Co-singer Baby Greensleeves was wont to give Max a blow-job during the song 'Blown Away Like A Fart In The Thunderstorm'. It was art born of soft porn and a rasp of Le Petomane.

Little wonder Splodge became the vanguard of the Punk Pathetique wing of Oi! Max upset some sensitive souls last year by launching the Rock Against Ginger movement, which (Max claims) saw him beaten up by gangs of red-headed yobs. I ask if he's had any dealings with that Texas Red fella Marty Robbins used to sing about, or indeed, anyone in possession of a "big iron" (no Halfin gags by request) but our conversation is rudely interrupted by a loud whooping arrival of Max's wizened old cleaner.

"She comes with the ranch," he says. "Funny woman, she's a Ku Klux Klan member." You're joking. Do you get on with her? "I got on her once. She weren't bad. Much better than talking to her."

A wizard between the sheets no doubt. Max hates racism, but attempting to talk to him about anything serious is like trying to nail ectoplasm to a ghost. Before I know it, he's banging on about a secret farm gig in El Paso. "The promoter didn't tell a soul," he claims. "He just filled the place with cows. He said he thought the music would soothe them but they stampeded...

"We went to see the Cartwrights too. What a waste of time. It was like flogging a dead Hoss." Ouch. Why did you really ditch the old band?

"I got fed up with 'em," he says. "I wanted to see what it would be like to mix pathetique ideas with a band who could really play." So now he has Ronnie Rocker on lead guitar, Tony Baloney on rhythm, Ricky Titcombe on drums and Willie Strang on bass – all originally of Great Yarmouth punk band The Crabs.

Max speaks passionately of his dream of putting together a Pathetique compilation, like the Oi albums, but for bands like the Notsensibles, the Postmen, the Pissflaps, the Gonads, Percy Thrower's Man-eating Plants and the Toydolls "as long as they don't keep sounding like Status Quo on sulphate."

He pauses. "I like Oi, but I prefer Pathetique," he says.

"Pathetique is being over-shadowed at the moment. We've got the same ideals as Oi, without the preaching. The preaching in Oi is getting a bit too much, we ain't gonna change the world. Our gigs are working class, but we're just having a laugh."

"We're not trying to sweep anything under the carpet, though," Willie interjects.

"Nah," says Max. "We've done that before. It's all dirt and fluff and Wavis O'Shave under there."

Postscript: 'Cowpunk Medlum' peaked at Number 69 in the UK charts. Max's record company immediately dropped him. Cow Punk was a beautiful dream but it wasn't to be. That wasn't the low-point of Max's story though. He went on to record the 'Delilah' ep with me as 'Max & Gal – The Brother's Gonad'. It was the worst-selling release in the histories of either Splodge or the Gonads. But we did have the grand-daughter of the fella who played Max in Hart To Hart on the cover, so our efforts weren't entirely wasted.

NO MADAM, THAT CHILD IS NOT MINE
Engelbert Humperdinck

Las Vegas, May 1995

THE first time I went to Las Vegas it was with ZZ Top, the second time it was with Engelbert; I'm not sure which visit was crazier. ZZ Top had the street cred, Engelbert had the women. Even at sixty, these randy old dames were throwing damp underwear – possibly Tena Lady Extra Plus – at him, along with room keys, flowers and love notes. It was extraordinary; not so much Viva as Saga Las Vegas.

He may be out of fashion for more than two decades, but here in the showbiz capital of the world, among the glamour and glitz of this gaudy gamblers' Mecca, the Hump still reigns supreme. Women of all ages flock to worship the Legend and his big throbbing ballads. At the show at Bally's Hotel and Casino, one swooning thirty-something shakes like Stevens with Parkinson's as the singer whisks her on to the stage. "Is your husband here?" he asks.

"Yes," she says, trembling.

"Pity," he grins.

"But," she whispers, "I'll be coming to see you in Denver without him..."

Engelbert is unfazed by the blatant come-on. Women have been offering themselves to him for 28 years. They've hidden in wardrobes, fainted at his feet, bitten him, allegedly borne his babies...Enge has had more paternity suits than stage suits, and is known to have paid maintenance for two now grown-up love children, Angelique and Jenna; their mothers being a California showgirl and, even sweeter, a Sunday School teacher from New York (talk about, "Thy rod and thy staff they comfort me"). He is said to know one phrase in eighteen different languages: "No madam that child is not mine." But that's not surprising, that's how you'd imagine the King of Romance to be. More surprising is the fact that Enge drives like a drunken sitcom Frenchman with a short attention span.

En route to Bally's from his favourite golf club, with me in the passenger seat, Enge swings between lanes, makes unorthodox turns, cuts people up and blames them...all while telling me tales about partying with Elvis. It's partly hilarious, partly surreal and entirely mind-boggling.

Even better, even in the midst of the Nevada desert Enge kept everything English. Before the show, in his dressing room, we sat there eating steak and chips, drinking pints of imported Ruddles ale (Iron Maiden's favourite tipple) and playing a game of darts. And he thrashed me! Engelbert hit the bull, he got three triple 20 – "one hundred and eighteeee" - with ease; he even finished on a double top. It was only later that he confessed that he was mates with darts legends Eric Bristow and Jocky Wilson...and has beaten them both.

There's only one other act I know who play darts before every show – AC/DC. And only one singer who drives as badly as he does – Bruce Dickinson from Iron Maiden. Bruce almost killed me, twice – once by driving the wrong way up a Florida slip-way into four lines of on-coming traffic, and then by throwing the Mercedes we were travelling in into reverse on the autobahn outside of Dortmund in Germany. But I digress.

THE next morning, over breakfast of bananas on dry toast, the last of the world class crooners stonewalls my attempts to elicit juicy gossip about his love-life. These days such talk gives Engelbert the hump - possibly because he knows my piece is ear-marked not for the rock press but for a salacious British tabloid.

"I've had a lot of adverse publicity," the Legend tells me. "It doesn't bother me but it's been hurtful to my family."

Maybe so but that didn't stop Pat his wife of 32 years and mother of the four children he owns up to – Louise, Jason, Scott, and Brad – once joking that he'd need to hire the Hollywood Bowl for a Father's Day party. Or the man himself once joking: "I see a fan's child and my first thought is, does that child look like me?"

"You only have one life," Engelbert notes sagely. "And in this business you're open to all manner of temptations. You have to accept that mistakes come and go past them. We've come through it all, my wife and I. She's a remarkable lady. She has tolerated me."

Pat was 16 when she fell for him; a looker "young, tanned with short, bubbly hair". He was 27 and a struggling dance band singer calling himself Gerry Dorsey. His actual name is Arnold George Dorsey. He was born in Madras, India, on May 2 1936; the son of a British Army engineer, the ninth of ten children. Enge was brought up Catholic and still keeps the faith.

When he was eleven, the family returned to Leicester, the Midlands city he still calls home. Chubby young Arnold started a paper round to pay for saxophone lessons. He left school at 15, worked for a while in a local engineering factory, did National Service in Germany, and then, after being demobbed, he started to sing in clubs. He made his stage debut in 1957 at the Bond Street Working Man's Club.

"I wanted to make it, that was my dream," he says. "To be somebody." It took a while. He performed for just £20 a night and half-starved for years. But at least the weight dropped off.

He changed his name to Gerry Dorsey, and waited seven years before marrying Pat. "I wanted to be able to afford to keep her." Their first marital home was a humble council flat in Hammersmith, West London where they got by on two meals a day - porridge for breakfast, mincemeat and mash for tea. Enge recalls:

"It had no curtains, no carpets, no light shades, nothing. Except love."

Salvation came in the shape of inexperienced songwriter turned showbiz manager Gordon Mills who was also born in India. Recognising his talent, Mills signed him up, and who changed his name to Engelbert Humperdinck after the composer of the fairy tale opera Hansel and Gretel. It may have been the most ridiculous name in pop but it was inspired. What comedian could resist it? The singer was said to have the first name that was worth 197 in Scrabble. They called him Pumper Nickel, Thumper Dick, Dumper Truck, Hump the Chump... yet it was a moniker that nobody ever forgot.

"Arnold didn't work as a stage name," he says. "Although it didn't do too badly for Schwarzenegger."

Mills was quite a talent spotter. He managed a Welsh lad called Thomas Woodward, whose name he changed to Tom Jones. He also wrote 'It's Not Unusual' for him...He later owned an exotic zoo at his home in Weybridge, Surrey. "Gordon said, 'Tom will be the rocker and you take the ballads," Enge recalls.

Engelbert's 1967 smash hit 'Release Me' had been hanging around the fag-end of the UK charts for weeks before entertainer Dickie Valentine fell ill and a prime slot became available on TV variety show Sunday Night At The London Palladium. It was the making of him. 'Release Me' went on to sell 15million copies worldwide, keeping the Beatles' 'Penny Lane' off the top spot and staying in the charts for more than a year. Girls started to scream whenever he appeared on stage. It was raining knickers every night...and Engelbert's management began pretending that poor Pat was his little sister.

It was time to move out of the council flat.

130million album sales later, the star has homes in Hawaii, Las Vegas, New Jersey, Los Angeles and, uh, Leicester...his vast Leicester mansion, built in 1856 for the Duchess of Hamilton, has tennis courts, a chipping green, a rose garden and its own pub. More super-hits followed: 'The Last Waltz', 'Spanish Eyes', 'There Goes My Everything' until it got to the stage that the star didn't need the Humperdinck. "I'll never forget the day my dincker fell off," he grins. "I think venues got tired of putting up all those letters. I've saved them a fortune by dropping it."

I didn't expect Engelbert to be funny; I thought he'd leave me railing against the perfumed effluence of old-school showbiz as kitsch and camp as it comes. But it's hard not to warm to the great ham. Enge sends himself up constantly; his stage show is packed with hilarious impressions – Elvis, Deano, Julio. He chats about meeting Prince Charles at a royal gala, and then, those mournful spaniel eyes twinkle and he says: "I'd just sung 'Release Me' and 'Secret Love' – I felt I should apologise and assure him it wasn't personal."

He met Elvis Presley here in Vegas, in 1967. "He came to see my show, he was an amazing guy. Most people shake hands but Elvis embraced me. He didn't take himself seriously. He was a humble man and we became friends. I last saw him six months before he died and he was a different man. He was pale and bloated, he seemed unhappy. Very sad."

To my surprise, Enge also performed with Jimi Hendrix – at the Finsbury Park Astoria in 1967, back in the days when the Hump sang 'Midnight Hour' in his set. "Jimi finished his set by setting fire to his guitar," the Legend recalls. "But he over-did it, there was a burst of flame a good ten feet high; they had to rush a fire extinguisher on stage and Jimi and the compere were both burnt."

I have only one burning desire, let me stand next to your fire...

Engelbert's own showbiz 'brush with death' came seven years later at the Houston Aerodrome in front of 73,000 paying customers. He'd decided to make his entrance on horseback, but the spotlight dazzled his mount. "The horse reared up and bolted across the arena," he recalls. "It tried to kill me! I clung on for grim death and eventually I got it to slow down. What a relief! Afterwards the promoters gave me the saddle."

LAS Vegas is all about re-invention. It was here, at the end of the 60s that Elvis, who had been buried by Beatlemania and the British invasion, re-emerged doing two shows a night to sell-out audiences at the Hilton. And the city has reinvented itself several times, turning from a humble railroad stop to a gambling town to a Mafia business centre (after Bugsy Siegel and Meyer Lansky built the Flamingo in the mid-40s).

No doubt the new Vegas hides hangovers from the old Vegas, but the city is all about entertainment and simple unpretentious pleasures now, whether your bag is playing one dollar blackjack downtown at Binion's, letting loose with a Magnum at the Gun Store or wallowing in showbiz nostalgia with the King of Romance. In this place where dreams become reality, reality is a box office dream for Engelbert's promoters. His retro cabaret show is packed out every night.

It's a growing market in a growing city. Vegas is unrecognisable from my first visit here with Top back in '83. Since then they've built O'Shea's, the Mirage, Excalibur, the Casino Royale, Treasure Island, MGM and the Hard Rock Hotel. Work has started on New York New York and Bellagio; they've built a $25million monorail between Bally's and the MGM which opens next month. It's booming. Vegas is expanding like Meatloaf's gut, the Clark Country gambling revenue has topped five billion a year, and old-style, irony-free showbiz blossoms in its munificent shadow. You can't beat the house, but the house still tries to send you away happy...

BACKSTAGE after the show, the Hump challenges me to another game of darts and wipes the floor with me again. But it feels better to know that he thrashed Bristow, Jocky Wilson and five other top dart players in his dressing room too. They were in Vegas for a tournament; they came to his show, enjoyed his hospitality and paid the humbling price.

Enge is certainly having a better time here than he had in Venezuela a couple of years back, when the narcotics squad poked machine guns in his back. "Customs officials thought I was carrying drugs," he says with a smile. "But they were just medical supplies – antibiotics, stomach pills, sleeping pills. I was locked up for six hours! I was behind bars singing 'Release Me'."

Nothing seems to ruffle the Lord of Lounge, except maybe his decades-long feud with Jones The Voice. After twenty years of fist-fights and sniping, Enge splashed out £1500 on a champagne meal with his old rival to try and make peace. Tom wasn't having any of it...

"It's a shame," he says. "We were pals early on, we had the same manager; we were like two great racehorses in the same stable. We should have been like Bob Hope and Bing Crosby, but it wasn't to be." Instead they were like the showbiz equivalent of Frazier and Ali, two rams who just can't stop butting heads. I tried to heal the rift, and we had a nice night, but that was it. We never socialized again."

He shrugs. What does it matter? He's got it all, a loving family, millions in the bank, a career he controls – he works two weeks on, two weeks off, to give himself time for golf and tennis and writing free verse poetry. And on stage, he's a superstar, a king.

I watch him sing 'Unchained Melody', and as he stretches out a hand a lithe blonde on the table next to me writhes like an eel. Yeah. He's still got it.

Postscript: Engelbert never reinvented himself as Tom Jones did. Sure cult BBC comedy hit The Fast Show used 'Release Me' as its theme tune and Enge's version of 'Fly High, Lesbian Seagull' on the sound track of Beavis & Butthead Do America takes some licking. But we'll pass over his Eurovision disaster. The great man has never been seen as cool. Not that he's complaining. These days the working class boy from an Army family can only reside in Britain for 90 days a year – for tax reasons.

The Legend still plays Vegas, where he owns Jayne Mansfield's old Pink Palace, and he still scans the crowd for young lookalikes every performance.

CRASS PURPOSES
Steve Ignorant

Marylebone, London July, 2014

STEVE Ignorant meets me in a Baker Street pub for a beer we both thought would never happen. Okay, make that beers...Crass fell out with me over thirty years ago when their posh-boy drummer Penny Rimbaud took umbrage at a positive but mildly piss-taking preview of their first release, which I'd written for Sounds. A war of words (and music) ensued, which culminated in an elaborate but failed sting when Crass secretly recorded a meeting they'd set up with me in a Covent Garden pub using anarcho-temptress Honey Bane as a honey trap...And yet here we are me and Steve face to face for the first time, getting on like Dial House on fire; just two working class Londoners shooting the breeze. It's a night of surprises, all right. Firstly because down-to-earth Steve shares my love of blue collar gag-tellers, secondly because his favourite band in the world are the Cockney Rejects.

"To me, the Rejects are the ultimate," he says. "Once I heard Stinky Turner's vocals I thought that if anything happened to me he could be the Crass front man because he had the same sort of voice and he means it. He screamed so hard he burst his dimples."

He smiles and adds: "My claim to fame is being drunk one night in France in this bar, shirt off braces down, standing on a table, glass in hand singing 'We Are The Firm'...I got thrown out for that. But as soon as I heard 'Where The Hell Is Babylon, can I get there on me bike?' I thought, that's the band for me. Because where was Babylon? Even Penny Rimbaud had a grin on his face.

"I always want to meet them, go down for a beer, but I heard they were a bit lairy, a bit trigger happy with their fists..."

And meet they did, happily, this year at Rebellion.

The man known originally as Steve Williams recounts the voyage of discovery that took him from the back-streets of Dagenham to the forefront of the global anarcho-punk movement.

"I was leaning out my bedroom window one Sunday afternoon while my Mum and Dad were snoozing off the dinnertime pub session and I listened to Vaughan Williams's The Lark Ascending on Radio 4," he says, eyes sparkling. "And I read a book called Kes...and I got sucked in..."

Both opened those sparkling peepers to a world beyond the life that had been mapped out for him by circumstance. At 12, he saw Saturday Night Sunday Morning, the film based on Alan Sillitoe's novel about a young machinist who wants more than the life his parents had. Steve identified with it immediately.

"The opening shot was just a bloke in a factory looking really tasty. And then he says: 'This lot got ground down before the war and they never recovered from it. I'm after a good time and the rest is propaganda.' And I knew that I wanted to be that, too, I wanted to dress up in a flash suit on a Saturday night."

Steve, who was born in Stoke on Trent, grew up with his grandparents, listening to the likes of Perry Como and Frankie Vaughan. Top Of The Pops let him experience other kinds of music. David Bowie was his first idol. He was "enormously" into him – until the Thin White Duke diverted into the blue-eyed soul of Young Americans. Later, even Crass's name would come from a Bowie lyric: 'the kids were just crass' ('Ziggy Stardust').

When Steve saw the Sex Pistols being interviewed on TV by Janet Street-Porter in 1976, "I thought, 'Yeah I want in to that'. It was the way that Johnny Rotten was on stage, his lairy-ness and how afterwards he said, 'That was really boring' and I thought I know what you mean, and that's what inspired me. That was punk. It was a feeling I think that came from the terraces."

At 17 he worked at a supermarket in Upton Park, East London, where they told him "do good for thirty years and you can become a counter manager..." He wanted more. His home life up to that point had been apolitical, conservative with a small 'c'. "Even though I grew up in Dagenham, I was ignorant about the trade unions and had only a quirky idea of what left and right meant. My politics came from books and films like Room At The Top" – the 1959 adaptation of John Braine's' novel about class and social climbing.

But then his older hippy brother took him to the Dial House commune where he met Jeremy Ratter, the philosopher and poet we know as Penny Rimbaud. Rimbaud was fourteen years older than Steve Ignorant but they had a shared love of punk, but a different interpretation.

"When Johnny Rotten sang 'I am an anarchist, I am the anti-Christ' I felt it sounded like a death knell," says Steve. "I wanted something more. Me and Pen formed Crass and I wrote a song called 'Do They Owe Us A Living', and then 'So What'. It was just the two of us at the start, then other people decided to join the band (we never invited them!). So instead of standing alongside Steve Jones from the Sex Pistols or Paul Simonon from The Clash, I'm next to some balding fat middle-aged hippy wearing a tank top with rainbow colours..." He grins and adds: "Now I can see where 'I wanna destroy' comes from...

"The other members of Crass were all older than me, they'd been to art school, been involved in the sixties radicalism, they were vegetarian; suddenly I was able to read poetry without anyone taking the piss...I'm meeting film makers, playwrights, and publishers. From being stuck in a bedroom in Dagenham I was meeting people telling to read Jack Kerouac, read the beat poets, read Last Exit To Brooklyn – they opened my eyes. I didn't mind that they were middle class, class was never an issue for me."

The magnificent Ruts were another of Ignorant's early favourites. But these were dangerous, politically confused and challenging times.

"When we started, we all wore black and we wore arm-bands. People started asking us to do gigs for the Young Communist League or the SWP and when we said, 'No, we're not political' they said, 'Ah, you must be rightwing'. Then we had the Erith slug squad asking us to do gigs for the Nazis, and when we said no they said 'You must be leftwing'. So we defined ourselves as anarchists, but because of the bombings connected to anarchism back then, to distinguish ourselves from the bombers, we put up a CND peace symbol too. The reason we had so many banners on stage was to stop people making the wrong assumptions about us."

Even Rock Against Racism disappointed him. "We played a RAR gig and the organiser came up at the end and gave us £2,000. We tried to give it back, but he wouldn't take it. We were shocked. This was supposed to be a benefit! I think we gave it to a donkey sanctuary or something like that."

Left and Right collided in Central London. "We had some British Movement boneheads turn up at our Conway Hall gig - not skinheads, not proper skinheads. One of the doormen leftwing got the SWP lot down, and it turned into a dirty big punch-up where everyone with short hair got it.

"We tried to talk to both sides. We were wrong. I think Conflict had it right – if someone comes to attack your gig, sort them out! Like the song says, 'You want to bash their heads in cos they've not got nothing in them'. Our problem was our audience were the weedy kids from villages and suburbia, the misfits. We couldn't ask our audience to do it but well done Conflict and the Cockney Rejects cos you got the boneheads out."

Crass touched the lives of tens of thousands worldwide without ever feeling the need to sell out. The band lived up to Paul Weller's line 'No corporations for the New Wave sons' by refusing to sign to a major label. They released their debut 12in, The Feeding Of The 5,000 on indie label Small Wonder and consistently kept the prices of their albums as low as possible, pioneering the 'Pay no more than...' stickers. Their attitude shook up the music business and shamed big companies into following suit.

The Mod Revival of 79/80 passed Steve by but he says "I thought they looked so cool. My partner is always telling me off for wearing a suit and cufflinks, but sometimes I just fancy dressing well. It's a Friday night tradition! The Jam stirred something up there, 'Going Underground' was a great song, 'Down In The Tube Station' - we've all been there."

Steve autobiography, The Rest Is Propaganda, co-written with Steve Pottinger has now sold out. "Because I'm more famous than you!" he laughs – and then pretends to be put out when a couple on an adjourning table clock me but don't know him from Adam. He goes on: "It was great working with Steve Pottinger because he wasn't a Crass fan. He didn't even know I was the singer."

Steve now lives in Norfolk, and when he isn't performing with Paranoid Visions he is part of the Palling Volunteer Rescue Service, working with the Coastguard and the RNLI rescuing folk from the perils of the North Sea. You can donate here: http://pallingrescue.co.uk/

He is clearly a man of integrity. Steve cares about people – and doesn't care much for authority. "There was a thing there called principles and I still have them," he says. "Don't just sit there and accept, question things. Even question Crass – we didn't always get it right."

WILD SEWERAGE TICKLES BRASIL
Squeeze

Charlton, London SE7, 2010

THEY'RE the coolest cats in pop, inspired song-writers with a string of enduring hits under their belts. But even Squeeze make mistakes. Chris Difford's foot-in-mouth moment happened on stage in Glasgow. "We'd just stepped off the plane at the end of an American tour," he recalls. "And I told the Scottish audience how good it was to be back in England..."

Glenn Tilbrook's personal nadir was far worse. He was on stage in Austin, Texas, when he realised he was losing a battle with his bowels. "I had a bad stomach upset and I had to go," he says, with an embarrassed smile. "I ran backstage with my guitar strapped on and just about made the cubicle. Unfortunately the guitar had one of those pickups that vaguely transmits sound ...I realised from the laughter in the wings when I got back that everyone had heard what was going on..."

Which brings new meaning to Squeeze songs like 'I Can't Hold On', 'Out Of Control' and possibly 'Wild Sewerage Tickles Brazil.'

Squeeze were made in Greenwich, South East London, 26 years ago, when local teenagers Chris and Glenn formed a band called Skyco with TV's Jools Holland and Paul Gunn. They got together after 15-year-old school-leaver Glenn spotted an ad Chris had put in a shop window in Blackheath Village which claimed 'Lead guitarist wanted for a band. Recording soon'. It was a blatant lie. There was no band and no contract, but the lads got on and decided to give it a go.

Within months they'd change their name to Squeeze and were incubating nicely on the lively local pub scene, alongside the likes of Dire Straits and the slightly less memorable Stone Cold Sober. By 1976 they were playing a three-nights-a-week residency at the Bricklayers Arms in Greenwich. The closest they got to a tour back then was a gig in New Cross. But punk kicked open the London club doors and with a 'New Wave' tag, Squeeze released their debut ep 'Packet Of Three' on the Deptford Fun City label.

Their first hit was 1978's Take Me I'm Yours. Fast forward a year and they'd gone Top Three twice with Cool For Cats and Up The Junction – both ditties imbued with local colour.

Three years on and Squeeze were headlining Madison Square Gardens. "I didn't feel my feet on that stage once," Chris smiles. "It was awe-inspiring. I'd never been introduced to 20,000 people at the same time before. It was electric. A lot of trousers were flapping around that day."

I FIRST met Chris in 1979, in his local, the Rose And Crown (known affectionately as the Lousy Brown) at the bottom of Croom's Hill, Greenwich, two minutes walk from his attic flat. He was by his own admission a serious drinker at the time and had written Cool For Cats in that very pub, taking inspiration from the duckers, divers and shady Romeos who constituted the clientele. Chris was looking 'slightly rough', as I recall. Understandably so. He'd just got back from three and a half months on the road in the US to find unwelcome squatters in his flat. "Fleas! They were everywhere," he moaned. "I had to have it disinfected and I've been decorating all day...I should have sued."

What was that about pop star glamour?

I'd taken my then wife along to meet him and Glenn, and Chris was immediately picking our brains about the cost of church nuptials. At 24, he was about to marry his US girlfriend and was planning two September weddings – one in the States and one in Greenwich, with a reception in the Albany. "With a couple of decent bands, a free drink every half hour, a stripper... You oughta come."

In the event, they only had one ceremony at St Alfrege's in Greenwich. The marriage lasted nine years; Chris's liver held out a little longer. A recovering alcohol, he gave up the demon drink in 1992 having drunk enough for two life times.

"We should have just got married in Vegas," he says ruefully when we catch up last month. "It would have been a lot cheaper."

We meet in Glenn Tilbrook's recording studio 45RPM on an industrial estate in Charlton, just around the corner from the Anchor & Hope pub where Squeeze played a low-key gig this summer and Glenn and I occasionally judge the talent show.

Difford moved out to an eight bedroom farm in Rye, Sussex, twenty years ago and now lives in a rented two-bedroom apartment in Hove with a downstairs studio. But Glenn never left out of the area and Chris admits London never left him.

"Even now, whenever I drive across Blackheath or I'm by the river, I feel a sense of home, a sense of belonging," he says. "This is where my roots are, this is where I feel comfortable."

WHEN I arrive Squeeze are rehearsing for the next night's gig at London's Hard Rock Cafe. They sound as tight as Joan Rivers's face in a wind-tunnel. Both seem as affable and easy-going as they had done in 1979. It was the band's richly observed local vignettes that first attracted me to them. Songs like It's Not Cricket could have been penned by Ian Dury, with lines like 'She used to do a topless/Down at the Surrey Docks/With tassels on her wotsits/She did a t'riffic job/Of raising all the...eye-brows/Of every lunch time mob'.

But the sheer brilliance of Up The Junction suggested that Squeeze were always destined to be more than just another parochial pub rock band. How many lives are mirrored by that tear-stained tale of young love broken by booze and the bookies?

Strip away the south east London earthiness and it's easy to see why they've been compared to Lennon and McCartney, Bacharach and David and even Rodgers and Hammerstein. Chris's witty lyrics coupled with Glenn's clever catchy tunes spell pure pop quality.

"That quote about Lennon and McCartney that the record company put on a sticker on the albums," says Glenn, slightly embarrassed. "It was just to open a few doors in the US for us. It meant there was more chance of getting played on the radio. That was all."

It was with another eye on the USA that Squeeze recorded their new 14 track Spot The Difference album. Glenn says "I went into my hotel room in New York, turned on the TV and saw a Heineken ad using our song 'Tempted'. It brought home to me that we don't own our own back catalogue. So we have no control about where and when our songs are used. So we recorded really good new versions of the old favourites that we can control."

Classics such as Pulling Mussels (From the Shell), Black Coffee in Bed, Another Nail in My Heart, Hourglass and Tempted are virtually indistinguishable from the earlier recordings because they were painstakingly recreated using much of the same equipment and recording techniques as the originals.

Slap & Tickle even uses the same mini-moog from 1979. And Glenn's vocals are stronger now, even if his ears are weaker...

Christopher Henry Difford was born on November 4th 1954. He attended West Greenwich Comprehensive School and worked in scrap metal yards, the building trade and lorry firm Hilton's before Squeeze took off. His London lyrics were moulded by those experiences.

"We'd started hanging around with some heavy characters. I'd worked down at Hiltons before so I knew what it was all about, but at the time it wouldn't have inspired me to write about it. Anyway, we got mixed up in that again in 1978 – people who run late pubs, y'know. We lived in a cocoon of pubs...But I exhausted that theme with the Cool For Cats album. You can only say so much about one aspect of life, and then it starts to get a bit of a bore."

He wasn't interested in writing about local politics, like all the blue collar jobs that have drained out the borough since the war either. Or the yuppification of Greenwich. Chris was more inspired by universal themes, by characters, story-telling, alcohol and infidelity...

Discussing Tempted, Chris says "being in a band is like being in the merchant navy - you see the world for a few years but there are women of easy virtue in every port of call and you have to behave yourself or go home with a guilty conscience, or worse - the pox." Asked what he went home with, Chris once confessed:

"A huge bunch of flowers...and a guilty conscience."

Booze has been a recurring, perhaps obsessive, theme, from celebration to the emptiness of alcoholism (Slightly Drunk, When The Hangover Strikes, The Great Escape, Tough Love, The Truth, There Is A Voice). Chris's words conjure up a vivid gallery of recognisable characters: 'The tick-tack man throws out his arms/his thin moustache stretched on his face' (Gone To The

Dogs); 'He has a crease in his jeans, a frown on his face/the scent of a man who thinks he has taste' (Cupid's Toy).

Glenn Martin Tilbrook was born on 31 August 1957 in Woolwich, London. You wouldn't have thought this easy-going guy was once a crop-haired, skinhead bad boy who got himself expelled from Eltham Green comprehensive school.

Naturally he supports the finest football team in London, Charlton Athletic FC and in 1998 Squeeze released Down In The Valley as a tribute. Glenn's passions are his studio – he's just had Nine Below Zero in recording – live performance, and the charity Love Hope Strength. His first marriage was also short-lived, ending around the time of his brief flirtation with heroin.

Glenn's writing partnership with Difford has lasted for twenty-six years, on and off, surviving numerous bust-ups and reunions en route. For him, Squeeze's greatest moment was their low-key1985 reunion gig in Catford. "Originally it was a pub gig for the crack, but during it we realized that perhaps we shouldn't have split up. To realise that was something else. There were about 80 people there."

Why did they split? Glenn shrugs. "We were doing everything we'd ever wanted and it was nothing like we thought it would be..."

He still has a burning need to play live. "I'd go mad if I didn't do a gig after a while," he says. "I'll play in practically any circumstances, so when we're not touring I'll just play in a pub. Usually the Anchor & Hope if we're not touring. I'll do anything that come to mind, mostly other people's songs but also a few Squeeze ones. The bedrock of the stuff I know are songs I learned when I was a kid - Beatles songs, Hollies songs, Monkees songs. I've always played Angel by Jimi Hendrix.

"I've always been the same. At the risk of sounding like a sickening child, I did actually used to go and knock on my neighbours' doors and sing for them when I was five."

As well as writing new material, Glenn and Chris plan to record an albums worth of freshly unearthed songs that they wrote in 1974! Glenn reveals: "Before we started gigging we spent a lot of time just writing and recording songs. A mate of mine, now a doctor, kept tapes of them, and they really stand up. Finding them and hearing them again was like going on a successful archaeological dig. Time Team for tunes! We want to record them as there were written, as a period piece. There is a whole set of songs about Trixie's, an imaginary nightclub inspired by Damon Runyon stories. We're starting work on that in the New Year."

WELL into their third decade together, Difford and Tilbrook are as keen to work as they ever were. And their place in pop's pantheon of greatness is generally recognised. In 2008, Mark Ronson presented them with the Ivor Norvello Award for Outstanding Contribution to British Music. While Lily Allen dubbed them "the Robert De Niro of music" when they received the Nordoff-Robbins Icon Award.

Neither star is as rich as they once were. "We had our golden-egg period, during Squeeze's heyday, years ago," says Chris. "But I over-spent like a Lottery winner. I loved spending money. It went on Concorde, fancy hotels, Maseratis...I went through a lot. I don't regret it, I don't think you should ever regret anything in life. I had fun while it lasted. What I'm trying to do now is lay another golden egg. That's the plan, at any rate." A golden egg. Let's hope they crack it.

JUST ANOTHER EX-GRAVEDIGGER INTO DADA
John Cooper Clarke

London, Soho. September 1978

ONE Tuesday in the office I was heard to remark, that I'd like to interview John Cooper Clarke.

"Okay," Alan Lewis said to me, but only if you do it in poetry…"

Well I jumped at the chance coz I thought I could crib from the naff rhyming nonsense of E. J. Thribb (17). Only trouble was, it was easy to see, Thribb didn't use enough imagery.

So I dug out my discs by the Manchester chap (only two singles if you wanna to be exact) and listened intently to inwardly digest…and went off to find him, now read the rest…

SAW THIS skinny guy in a polka-dot shirt and sunglasses being pursued by a squad of Chinese waiters through Soho. He dodged into my doorway, grabbed me by the shoulders and garbled "Can't go back to Salford, the cops have got me marked." That was it. Re-enter the waiters, exit Johnny Clarke…

John Cooper Clarke, known nationally as the punk poet, is a nervous, lean streak from Salford who has found fame via the new wave but has been going much longer. He's not your usual media image scribe content with sedate Book Club renderings of polite heady verse for polite heady people. 28 years old and thoroughly working class, his poems are vividly forceful surrealistic diatribes steeped in pop culture, libertarianism and music hall comedy, all delivered in harsh Mancunian tones.

In a soulless CBS office and later at a typical 'grease, grease or grease' caff ("Hot dogs direct from Crufts, done in diesel oil") Clarkey came clean about his wretched past.

"Poetry's a thing I've always done but I've not always made a living out of it," he says in a voice that would be more at home in the Rovers Return. "I worked on the docks as a fire-watcher, had a few extra-legal occupations…I was a window cleaner, a grave-digger – they said 'You haven't got any objections to working with spades have you?' I said no, not at all. 'Right,' they said 'Get digging.'

"I'm a dosser again now, but I'm not on the dole...I signed off the Nat King Cole when I came down here." He goes on: "I was doing similar poetry before punk, but punk has opened up more exciting gigs. Jazz clubs and pubs are all right but they're not so much of an event as new wave gigs. It was more or less reading while people are eating chips.

"I've written loads of stuff but the stuff I perform at gigs tends to be a certain type which isn't always the kind of poem that I write, but I'm only really interested in poems that get an immediate response. That's what I'm interested in doing on stage, as opposed to kind of more esoteric stuff."

Poems that have built up a large working class audience even if the 'immediate response' isn't always favourable..."I've got the largest collection of broken glasses in Britain," he laughs. "They're all mounted on little plaques at home: 'Lyceum, March', 'Vortex, December'..."

ED Banger suffered the same fate at the Lyceum, and, I expect, Jilted John would have done four months ago (the blind injustice of it all). Talking of suffering, was the b-side of the new single Kung Fu International – where our hero is set upon by a balding embryonic Bruce Lee outside a Chinese take-away – based on real life?

"Oh aye, yeah, I got jumped in Wally Range. It was half a dozen blokes; they gave us a severe pasting then discovered I was the wrong geezer..."

Kung Fu International is more representative of the stage Clarke, stripped of musical backing. The a-side, Post War Glamour Girl, is recited over a disco beat which wasn't favourably received by the critics...

"Yeah, it's completely different to what I've been doing, but all this 'signs to a record company, they make him go disco' stuff isn't true; it wasn't like that at all. CBS didn't have anything to do with the production of the single or the LP, it's all my fault."

The album, tentatively titled Bins And Hooters is due out in October and John says "a lot of it's like the single as opposed to the Innocents EP which was pretty doomy. It's been mixed for day time listening. There's Readers Wives, Valley Of The Lost Women, Tracksuit, Health Fanatic, I Married A Monster From Outer Space, I Was A Teenage Werewolf, oh, and a couple of live tracks too, Salome Malone and a live version of Psycle Sluts."

There's an obvious US influence, and Clarke, a huge Elvis fan, readily admits to being hooked on Septic culture ever since he saw his first Dean Martin and Jerry Lewis movie. Before punk he'd tried to make it on the cabaret circuit performing in Manc clubs like the Piccadilly and the Embassy. After surviving a Bernard Manning audience, what a fear could the Slaughter & The Dogs crowd hold for him?

Do you ever use a backing band live?

"Well I did one and a half gigs with the Curious Yellows, but not usually. I think I'd like to do some gigs with a group, say maybe two distinctly separate sets."

I Married A Monster has an anti-racist vibe. "Yeah, that's the kind of theme that runs through it. I don't like to put one sort of meaning on anything, not even on poems that are as one-dimensional as that. But yeah, that's the apparent theme that runs through that one, racialism, extending it to intergalactic regions. Racist attitudes in the Space Age are really anachronistic aren't they? You're exploring other planets and people still can't get on with somebody in Africa...

"Action Man is about the link between impotence and the need for violence, probably, because Action Man, as you know, has got all the equipment except genitalia. Quite meticulously completed by craftsmen."

How about Post War Glamour Girl? "That's sort of a mongrel. I hate talking about poems, specially that one, which is loosely hinged on the glamour theme – the way women are pictured as opposed to the way they actually are, and the way men are supposed to react to pictures of women in certain scenarios, the tiger rug and the telephone. I've got this pack of nude playing cards on me that I got from this joke shop that were sort of knocked up in the 50s, and the 50s idea of what is glamorous is completely different to today's..."

Not that corsets should ever go out of fashion...

"Health Fanatic is my latest poem, it's about the keep-fit trend, the sort of people who run at the sides of busy roads in the vain belief that they're getting healthy when in actual fact they're breathing in eighty times more lead than anyone else. Deep breaths with their mouths open, and all this diesel is going down their throats... They'll probably joss it next year. If they took it easy they'd have probably been alright..."

I remember when we were about 13 we used to buy health magazines...

"Oh aye, Health & Efficiency, H & E. At one time it was the only magazine you could ever get to see pubic hair in. It's kinda taking advantage of nudists, magazines like that. It's a bit like exploiting children in a way...I've written a lot about pornography, it's a bit of an obsession really."

Bred of a misspent youth perched over Men Only?

"Yeah, but not only that sort of pornography, soft porn gets me an' all. Asexual pornography. I think it's very strange, asexual pornography. It's like a daft thing to want to do. I think the last thing pornography should do is make sex appear like it isn't dirty. I think it'll make people impotent, that attitude, eventually. Like Woody Allen says, 'sex is only dirty if you're doing it right'."

Allan Konigsberg, Lenny Bruce, Ian Dury and Lord Buckley, the British hipster comedian who made it in the States, are all name-checked in JCC's list of acknowledged influences, along with Mickey Spillane, pop music, pulp sci-fi, television, movies, dada and anarchism. His Dad, a gambler and a naturally funny man, was an influence too. The poets who first ignited his passion were a far cry from the Salford slums, though.

"The first poetry I ever sort of read and was actually excited by was the futurists. Poets like D'Annunzio and Marinetti. Actually they were fascist poets as it happens, they later aligned with Mussolini, but I'm not into that part of it. They were the first poets I read who used hard imagery, lots of it, spread it all over. Of the surrealists, I love the painters. I like Rene Magritte especially and Dorothea Tanning as well. She was really great, very erotic her, and Leonor Fini. I like Dali..."

Shame he got so cosy with Franco...

179

"He's sort of apolitical, him. But he used to do stuff for Franco and his family. I just don't think he's at all interested in that sort of aspect of it, he'd probably say he was apolitical. Well he wouldn't say that, he'd probably say something that'd really baffle you. But I think he's coming from an apolitical direction which is something I'm cynical of. I think an apolitical stance is a political stance. Me, I'm bigoted, I'm biased. There are whole sections of the population that I just put in a bag and say 'He was bound to say that, he's rich.'

"I see myself as having left-wing attitudes, also libertarian attitudes. But I'm not overtly into politics and I'm not into sloganeering at all. I'm really suspicious of slogans, they're like adverts, they make people act without thinking."

THERE was a whole link up with surrealism and Trotskyism in the twenties wasn't there? I ask, taking the conversation into areas most rock writers fear to tread.

"Andre Breton was a personal friend of Leon Trotsky, and Trotsky himself was very interested in the art of the time. Well of course when it went off in Russia, Dada happened at almost exactly the same time. Tristran Tzara, the fellow who sort of invented Dada poetry was writing in Geneva just as Lenin was leaving there for Russia. And with Trotsky, he wasn't just a propagandist, his work is creative writing in its own right."

Truly, which is why it's surprising that most 'orthodox' Trotskyites are a colossal pain in the harris. But if this conversation is baffling you and the nearest you've got to surrealism is Monty Python or your own dreams, get hold of Bomb Culture by Jeff Nuttall, probably the best intro to rebel culture around. Nuttall quotes a US surrealist group who defined rebel poetry as 'breathing like a machine gun, exterminating the blind flags of immediately reality...' Clarke's metaphor of choice would more likely be a pea-shooter followed by a clown's custard pie in the kisser.

His poetry is far more accessible, he's not the sort of 'artist' the middle class will easily stuff into Southbank museums-come-mausoleums. But hold on, 'Cooper Clarke' that sounds a bit posh, old chap? Are you a slumming aristocrat on the quiet?

"No, it's not hyphenated. Cooper is like Charlie or Harry, just me middle name. I adopted the Cooper because at one time there was this other geezer called John Clarke going round reading poetry at the same time. Talking of names I was interviewed by this geezer in Plymouth once called Robin Bastard. That was his real name, Robin Bastard. He was a rich kid, his dad owns most of Plymouth, Lord Bastard, that's a great name for an aristocrat that, innit? You can tell he didn't get his money the hard way…"

We're in the cafe now, chewing the grease, with John coming out with outrageous sayings like "Jonathan King ought to be strangled in his bed alongside the Royal Family", which puzzled me – what is ugly-bug pop irritant King doing in bed with the Royals? But before I can ask John has moved on.

"This is the sort of thing that influences me," he says, clutching the menu. "Things that read from top to bottom. Look at that, 'Steak and kidney pud and two veg, 70p' – what a dynamite one-liner."

What's that album title mean again? I ask in a desperate bid to bring him back to here and now.

"Bins is slang for glasses, binoculars, don't you use it down here?" Of course we do. We talk a bit about London slang. "I find rhyming slang is used more in Manchester than it is here," he says.

"It's always been big coz you can make your own up, it's great. Northern rhyming slang you probably wouldn't get down here, like Mather & Platt which is a large engineering firm in Manchester, it means twat. There's bottle of acker, Acker Bilk, milk…"

Fancy a pig's ear?

"That seems like a good idea…"

MUSIC TO MARCH TO
Crisis

Brighton, September 1978

"WHAT have we got? FUCK ALL!"

Five hundred throats fracture Brighton's balmy seaside calm, five hundred angry fists punch the sky. "What have we got? FUCK ALL!"

The portly police inspector is not impressed.

"The next time anyone swears, this constable will arrest you," he says in a clipped tone, his face as red as a boiled lobster. Unabashed, a cheeky Scouse voice rings out: "What have we got?" And the crowd roar back "EFF ALL." Everyone laughs except the portly cop who looks almost as embarrassed as the majority of delegates filing into the Trade Union Congress this overcast Tuesday afternoon.

The noisy orange-jacketed army of punks, skinheads and street corner yobs opposite are a noisy irritation, shattering the peace of the Brighton promenade with their high-decibel demands: "What do we want?" "THE RIGHT TO WORK!" "When do we want it?" "NOW!"

They're also an unwanted reminder of the scourge of youth unemployment. Official figures say that there are 1,608,000 on the dole in the UK; 441,000, more than a quarter of them, are under twenty. There are whole generations who will never know work.

Of course we all know people who work and sign on, or sign on every week and drop out. But you also know school-leavers who desperately want to find employment, just to be able to live a little, to feel good about themselves and hold their heads up.

They're the kids who die a bit inside every time they hear the words, "Sorry, vacancy filled." The Giro Generation. That's who the protesters say they're fighting for, that's whose ranks they are mostly drawn from. Statistics made flesh.

These marchers have come from all over the country, but Glasgow's self-styled Sham Army are the liveliest and the loudest ("not a fan club, we're a street army that supports their songs").

182

BACKTRACK three days to Saturday, 2nd September, and the start of the protest. Marchers assembled outside Bethnal Green Hospital in East London where the staff were staging a work-in to save the hospital from closure. The march has been organised by Rock Against Racism, the Campaign Against Youth Unemployment (linked to the Young Communist League) and the Right To Work Campaign (often said to be a front organization for the Trotskyite Socialist Workers Party, about whom more later.)

The protest has attracted teenagers from all over the UK who are given orange Right To Work jackets to wear. These are quickly covered with felt-tip graffiti: 'Career Opportunities – The Clash', '1977 was last year's thing', 'Manchester United FC', 'Pogo On A Blister', 'Sham 69', 'Piss Artists Against The Nazis', 'Elvis Lives', 'West Ham', 'Mekons', 'Celtic', 'Lurkers' and various other groupings against the Nazis, including Beans, Cockneys, Muppets, Sooty & Sweep and perhaps most unexpectedly, Genesis. A representative of 'rock against Selling England By The Pound' perhaps.

RAR has organized the music for the day, and it's a proper red-fist racket. First up, playing on the back of a lorry are Crisis, a young punk band from the Weller-kissed streets of Woking, Surrey, who are so determinedly political that before I saw them live four months ago they had only ever been written about in the far-Left press. And yeah, they're committed but they aren't playing at being rebels. If anything they recall early Sham: their songs are simple and muscular, the lyrics pour from the heart and the gut, and their stance is as punk as you can get.

Jimmy Pursey once said of Crisis: "They're good but they're Commies ain't they?" I put that charge to them today. Commies?

"Not if you mean Russia," says skinhead bassist Tony Wakeford, 19, a little disingenuously. "But a couple of us are socialist and the others are anti-racist. That's why we're playing this march, because unemployment is the worst breeding ground for racism.

It's good that there are punks and skins on the march, not just boring lefties."

Their uncompromising stance has seen Tony get battered by British Movement neo-Nazis, and the band banned from hometown clubs for being "too political". Step Forward records allegedly got cold feet about signing them for the same reason, so the group is considering signing to San Francisco label Heavy Manners who also manage the Dils of 'I Hate The Rich' fame.

"The Dils are the group we have the most in common with," says rhythm guitarist and contrarian Doug Pearce. "They raised $4,000 for the US miners. I don't think there are any other genuinely political punk bands around; even the Clash deny it now."

The motto of Doug's old school (West Byfleet secondary modern) was 'Deeds Not Words'. It's a maxim Crisis live by, devoting hours of their time to working class causes. Today, they cope well with the constant whirr of the generator and the lurching stop-starts of the lorry which they're sharing with four fierce female fans known as the Effects Of Crisis, led by Lu Malicious and Fleshy Parts, with roadies Martin and Flea. Their best songs are the older ones – direct and forceful numbers such as Search & Destroy (about last year's bloody Lewisham riot designed to stop a National Front march) and their soothing anthem Kill, Kill, Kill.

The newer numbers are different: slower but solid and deliberately not as catchy. Perverse bastards. "We were getting too poppy," Doug explains. "People were coming along to our gigs just for the music, so we wrote some heavier material. Our new stuff resulted from the sort of gigs we do too – it's music to march by."

White Youth was written to a marching rhythm and ends with the chant of 'We are black/We are white/Together we are dynamite.' Apt. At Brixton, Crisis pack away their gear and RAR's reggae stalwarts Misty In Roots take over.

Tony, like the rest of the group, is signing on; he decides to stay on the march and walks the rest of the way wearing an unnecessary Chelsea scarf. The more we march, the more people relax about singing. The sun is on our side (if not The Sun) and the donation collectors are doing a good trade with bystanders who either smile supportively or look bemused. Very few are hostile. With Misty stirring us on with good old homegrown alien rhythms, I decide to get the goods on RAR and collar Irate Kate of Temporary Hoarding fame.

It's about two years since Rock Against Racism first saw the light of day. In that short time, RAR has built up 52 functioning support groups and, to the frustration of many a public spirited bog cleaner, shifted close on 150,000 stickers, which if nothing else have provided a welcome change from the usual uninspired 'Gordon 4 Sharon' or WHUFC graffiti blighting the khazis of the nation's seedier establishments.

The RAR publication, Temporary Hoarding, which I'm proud to have written for, is an impressive punkoid combination of news, views, reviews and organisation. Since the collapse of Mark Perry's Sniffin' Glue, TH surely ranks as the country's biggest selling street music magazine, shifting more than ten thousand copies per issue. But RAR's main claim to fame has been its live shows, ranging from small discos via club gigs to the stunning success of Carnival – set up in partnership with the Socialist Workers Party-driven Anti Nazi League.

Of course this has led to accusations that RAR is also a front for the SWP. Irate Kate (actually 18-year-old Kate Webb) is RAR's first paid worker, and she sighs audibly when I put the charge to her.

"I don't know how many times we've got to say it, but RAR is completely independent," she says. "I'm not an SWP member, other people aren't, in fact most aren't. The main people who run RAR now in London are kids who've come out of punk and whose political commitment only goes as far as RAR."

I know this anyway because I was working at the Socialist Worker when RAR was dreamt up by Roger Huddle, a print worker there, and actor activist Red Saunders. Both were SWP members.

"We're completely financially independent, though," Kate insists. "Anyone who wants can come and look at our books. We work with anyone who's anti-racist, even the Young Conservatives. Our mistake was that the first mailing address we used was an SWP address, but that's because it was the only place we could get to use as premises."

I ask Glaswegian punk Big Frankie, 19-year-old Frank Rafferty, why he's marching. "Because I'm fucking sick of these people at the TUC," he says with venom. "Half of them have got two or three jobs on company boards; they don't know what it's like in the real world. I'm a scaffolder and I've been unemployed for four months since I got laid off. Before that I was out of work for a year."

How many jobs have you applied for?

"Too many, and not all in the building trade either. Glasgow is one of the worst places for unemployment in Western Europe. I'm no bloody scrounger. The real scroungers are down there in Brighton."

Big Frankie puts a human face on unemployment figures blandly parroted by establishment politicians. But is he and kids like him just being used by far-Left groups?

March 'Daddy' John Deason is the secretary of the Right To Work Campaign; he also happens to be a Central Committee member of the very same SWP. "Like all working class initiatives there are politically active people involved," Deason parries, when I put the exploitation charge to him. "The SWP has made major efforts to build this campaign and the Anti-Nazi League. But many other people with other views are involved including leading members of the Labour Party, like Ernie Roberts" – Roberts launched the ANL with Paul Holborow, another SWP Central Committee member in May last year.

The cynical response is simple: if this situation was reversed, if the NF had set up an umbrella organization and involved a few Tory backwoodsmen as window dressing, the SWP would be furiously denouncing it as a fascist front.

Deason doesn't see it. "This march has been financed and sponsored by more than a thousand trade union organizations," he says calmly. "If you think they're all SWP fronts, then that's very flattering to the SWP but it's not exactly true to life. The biggest 'organization' on this march is people who aren't in any organization."

A former AEU shop steward in Warrington, John talks more about the crippling effect of the Labour government's Social Contract on the working class's willingness to fight. But our conversation is gleefully interrupted by the Glasgow kids armed with megaphones: "And here we are at Ladbrokes for the John Deason stakes, and it's 5-1 he'll get charged today with genocide, 12-1 it'll be for crippling fifty coppers while resisting arrest..."

Every year, Deason gets nicked on various charges and later cleared. This year he wasn't. They got Big Frankie instead.

MONDAY morning I drive down to meet the marchers again with Tom Robinson and Syd and Ruth from RAR. Tom's entirely middle class and a little unworldly but he appears to be a genuine and sincere guy. He won't appear at the London or Brighton ends of the march because he doesn't want to steal their thunder, he says.

Some of the tough little tearaways aren't pleased to see him, calling him a "poofy cunt" under their breath. But that's before he performs an intimate one-man set for them, winning every one of them over.

Tom stands beneath a tree lit up with arc lamps, surrounded by marchers, and plays his twelve-string until he can play no more: We Can Swing Together, I Shall Be Released (for George Ince – the Tom Robinson Band has supported the campaign to prove his innocence since they began), Don't Bogart That Joint from Easy Rider, and new numbers including the heartfelt Blue Murder about the death in police custody of Liddle Towers, an electrician from County Durham. These pave the way for an emotional, but crowd-dividing Glad To Be Gay, that is followed by calls for Grey Cortina ("I can't do that on an acoustic," said Tom, but he does) and Winter Of '79 ("I can't do that on an acoustic" – but he does that too).

Tom even lends his guitar to Mick O'Farrell, a Man U supporting marcher from Hatfield, who wrote his own set of funny, telling songs and poems while he was doing bird for football hooliganism in Pentonville prison. Tom returns for Walk On The Wild Side with John Deason coerced into becoming Pointer Sister in chief on backing vocals, and then the Glasgow mob take over for a version of Sham's If The Kids Are United with lyrics of their own: 'We've marched from Glasgow and Burnley too/Our feet are blistered through and through/We marched for miles and we all agree/It's time we took over from the TUC/IF THE KIDS....'

This segues into a passionate rendition of You'll Never Walk Alone with everyone on their feet, fists clenched with Tom, for Tom, for the march, the cause and for each other. Robinson's set has acted like an electric charge; blisters are forgotten as kids conga around the campsite chanting: 'TUC is tragic/Right to Work is magic la-la la-la'. People sing every song they know for hours. I even contribute my own rendition of Mother's Lament, a ditty so said it'd squeeze a tear out of a glass eye. Especially with my singing voice...

TUESDAY: the marchers reach the TUC conference just after midday and all the spirit of last night and the frustration of being who and what they are spills over into angry, full-blooded chants and songs. It has been an anger march, not a hunger march, and that fury is now fired point blank at the delegates who are party to this New Jerusalem of wage cuts, closures and dole queues.

Some of them clench fists in solidarity, other sneer or just try to ignore the whole thing as if they're embarrassed to be reminded of the real world. Smug old men who have sold out every ideal they might once have had. How does it go, Joe? 'They're all fat and old, queuing for the House of Lords...'

"Unemployed, we are here, wo-oh, wo-oh!" chant the marchers. "We'll throw Len Murray off Brighton pier, wo-oh/Who are we? Giro Kids! Fighting for the right to live, wo-oh, wo-oh-oh, wo-oh.'

A little later, Denis Healey turns up grinning, and then PM James Callaghan arrives in a limo and slips in the back, Tom Driberg style.

"Labour isn't working, the Tories never will," the marchers yell. A kid from Burnley, Lancashire, spits on the floor. "It sickens you when the party you've been brought up to believe in stabs you in the back," he says.

"I dinna know aboot that," replies Johnny, a young Scottish punk. "All I know about is punk rock and fighting the Tories and the fucking snobby bastards."

Two marchers slip into the conference hall and start heckling Callaghan who promises to get them both jobs and then does a vanishing trick worthy of Paul Daniels at the end of a summer session.

When TUC General Secretary Len Murray leaves with a police escort, the demo surge forward to talk, argue, anything... the thin blue line pins back the front line firmly. The kids retaliate by pogoing on the spot singing "We're only doing our job" repeatedly.

At around 4pm we hear that five of the Glasgow punks have been nicked on suspicion of shop-lifting. The heavens open and it pisses buckets.

Later I get the train back to London while the marchers re-assemble at the local bus garage to see sets from local bands the Piranhas, the Smartees, the Distructors and East London punk folk bard Patrik Fitzgerald.

Patrik stays on for the next day and attempts to play an evening set on the beach, contravening a local by-law. In the ensuing row, twelve more marchers are nicked and one young girl reportedly has her arm broken.

Back home, the weekend is already a mental blur. But certain images will stay with me for a long while. Like Mick O'Farrell reciting his Chairman Of The Bench poem, Tom Robinson's campsite performance, Tony Wakeford pathetically refusing to try and bribe me with beer. Then there's the sense of camaraderie, the communal sharing of booze and fags, the anger outside of the conference, the instant songs and terrace style chants. But it's not the new numbers that sum up the march for me, or even the punks and skins singing Career Opportunities and If The Kids Are United. No, the song that sums up the march for me was sung around midnight on Monday by a log fire by a short Geordie girl, and sung again by everyone else every day after that. It's an American folk song that stems from the bad old days but looks forward to better ones to come. It's a conversation between a wife and husband that goes:

'"Oh why don't you work like other men do?"/"How the can I work when there's no work to do?/Hallelujah, I'm a bum/Hallelujah bum again/It'll take a revolution to revive us again".'

Postscript: Crisis split in 1980 and re-emerged a year later as Death In June; some observers claimed that the name, based on the Nazi night of the long knives, was either a tribute to the revolutionary Strasserite strand of Nazism or a flirtation with fascism. Douglas Pearce rejects the charges but refuses to address the question directly saying variously that people should decide for themselves and that his lyrics are shaped more by his homosexuality than political concerns. Crisis never got paid by RAR, not even for expenses they incurred when they had to hire in PAs because inexperienced local promoters had forgotten to do so. Tony Wakeford, at the time of this article a card-carrying member of the SWP, went on to join the National Front – something he deeply regrets; he now performs in a neo-folk band called Sol Invictus. Crisis drummer Luke Rendall ended up in Theatre Of Hate with Kirk Brandon but was reportedly murdered in the Noughties.

'Fleshy Parts' was Virginia Turbett who became a freelance photographer working mainly for Sounds. Don't ever call her Fishy Parts because it really pisses her off.

Mick O'Farrell became a founder member of the now defunct revolutionary socialist and fiercely anti-fascist Red Action faction. Mick's poem Chairman Of The Bench was printed on the inner sleeve of the fourth Oi! album, Oi Oi That's Yer Lot, and Red Action organized many Oi Against Racism shows. Some Red Action members were heavily involved with the IRA and two were jailed for their part in the Harrods bombing. Other former Red Action activists went on to form the Independent Working Class Association.

Rock Against Racism fell apart in the early 1980s. All of its books, archives and photos were destroyed by an arson attack on Red Saunders's photographic studio in 1991.

Tom Robinson had his last hit single with 'War Baby' in 1983. He is now a BBC Radio 6 DJ; he married a woman and has two kids.

ARE YOU DRINKING WHAT I'M DRINKING?
The Blood

IT'S 2.47am in the studio and we've completely run out of beer. Maybe time to knock it on the head, you might think. But you're not The Blood. Jamie, the guitarist JJ Bedsore, spots that the cleaning fluid used on the mixing desk contains isopropyl alcohol. He gets five cups and some flat Coke from the kitchen and the party, sorry, serious work of finishing the album continues.

Drinking was the bedrock of the Blood, and the cirrhosis of their career. My favourite memory comes from when I was managing them back in 1984 – 5 and had put them on at the Walthamstow Royal Standard. As we were knocking back a few light ales after the set, I asked who their designated driver was for the night. Casually, singer Colin Smith, aka Cardinal Jesushate, gestured towards a table. "He is," he said with a grin. And there was one of their roadies spark out on the floor, his face down in a pool of his own drool.

"You're the most sober one here, Gal," Colin continued. "You'd better drive us." Which is how I, who only drove an automatic at the time, found myself driving a lorry load of lashed-up lunatics with Jamie changing the gears. By some miracle I got us all back to Charlton without incident (unless you're being picky and think me driving straight over one small roundabout counts…)

Ah, The Blood. What a band. They were like a cross between The Damned, Alice Cooper and the Stranglers with a real flair for writing anthems: Stark Raving Normal, Mesrine, Megalomanic (about the Pope), Gestapo Khazi…everyone a gem, blessed with splenetic guitar and massive choruses. They should have been huge. But the Blood had everything going for them except a work ethic. They wanted to scam their way into the charts at a time when scams were exhausted.

The route to success was solid gigging I told them sternly and got road manager Brian Collinson to book a van for a UK tour. The band were so dead set against working that they immediately sprayed "Fuck off you cunts" and similar pleasantries over the outside of the van and frequently pissed out of the back of it in a bid to get nicked. They would rather have spent a week in the cells

191

than on the road. But the long arm of the law eluded them. As did the success their talent deserved.

I did collude in a few scams. I put an appeal in the agitprop pages of City Limits urging feminist sisters to come and picket the sexist bastards whose favourite trick was to fill a blow-up doll with butcher's offal and take a chainsaw to it on stage. And they did! (The dolls were supplied by my old mate Si Spanner who had a sex shop in Soho, in return for getting on their guest list when they played the Marquee etc).

On another occasion I encouraged them to write a satirical Geldof-skewering number post Band Aid entitled Still Looking After Number One but they split up before it could be released.

Jamie died on 20th July 2004, aged just 44, from multiple organ failure. His parents had died and he'd basically drunk himself to death with the proceeds from the sale of their house in Shooter's Hill...

Here are some memories from a happier time...

Blood Brothers

Covent Garden, June, 1983

"IT'S all noise, innit?" quicksilver swift guitarist JJ Bedsore shrugs over a foaming Kembles Head pint. "Raucous noise."

"Yeah, lairy noise," agrees Cardinal Jesus Hate, the Blood's crazy-eyed vocalist, a smouldering cauldron of wit, shit and outrage. "We don't write a song to fit any category."

"We're just tuneful and LOUD," JJ continues. "We'll always be gutsy. Any song we write will always have that Marshall sound cranked right up. We're like a fusion of punk and rock, shock rock. There doesn't have to be a distinction."

We're discussing where music is going in this strange world where punk has split into rival factions, and the differences between different types of sulphate-charged rock are blurring. Punk-metal hybrids have been discussed in the press; it's a mixed marriage that could give birth to a new scene devoted to nothing less than Total Noise! The Blood have the skill to fit the bill but "heavy metal audiences are too laid back," says the Cardinal, or Colin as his Mum knows him.

"A lot of our songs are a bit too tuneful for most metal," JJ, aka Jamie, continues. "You don't get a lot of metal bands who use minor chords" – a claim that suggests he hasn't heard much Iron Maiden. "We don't look Heavy Metal either, but our songs are too intricate musically for punk."

The Charlton boys embark on some dangerous dissing of other contemporary bands. JJ sneers at Twisted Sister: "I can't see what the big deal is about wearing make-up. Everyone wants to make money but it just seems to me that they're trying too hard. What did you call them? Dockers in drag! Ha! Still Mary Quant sales will rocket. And that's another thing – they don't drink!" He shakes his head at this alien concept, before adding contemptuously:

"They probably don't want to get lipstick on their glasses."

The Anti-Nowhere League? "They've got a brilliant tasty image," JJ allows. "But they just can't play. They're like GBH, they look right but they ain't got the music to back it up. What do they do that's outrageous apart from throw in a few fucks?"

How about the Exploited? "The guitarist and bassist are good geezers," says Colin. "If they got rid of Wattie they'd be a lot better off. He's just a big-headed scumbag. Up north he had about five cans of beer on stage and all he was doing was getting a mouthful and gobbing it over everyone. I couldn't believe, good beer wasted when we were skint…"

Will they be skint for long though? The Blood's devastating debut ep Megalomania is the single of the year so far, the most impressive first release since Blitz's All Out Attack ep. The song, which targets Papal hypocrisy has whizzed straight into the Indie Top Ten. It's a blistering whirlpool of energy, aggression and MELODY; an atheist anthem of Pistollian proportions.

"I hate the Pope and everything he stands for," the Cardinal shrugs. "But that song is dedicated to religious maniacs of all denominations. If God were here now, I'd boot him in the bollocks for the misery and human suffering perpetrated in his name."

Regular readers of the Sounds gossip column Jaws will recall that Colin recently paid an early morning call on his local Charlton priest claiming to be under the influence of "lairy spirits". It was after he'd started the exorcism rites that the Cardinal revealed the spirits in question went by the names of Jim Beam and Johnny Walker. And if you think that's shocking, Colin just told me he was voting Conservative! Blimey, run that up the flagpole and see who salutes it! Why Maggie, Col, because you're committed to deregulation and free enterprise? "Nah," he says. "It's cos I want to stay on the dole."

The Blood are the bastard sons of Alice Cooper and The Damned with a pinch of Derek and Clive and a mole or two from Lemmy's hideous boat-race thrown in for good measure. Their heroes include The Who, Ozzy and Alex Harvey, musicians who "had good tunes and an out of order edge".

Colin explains: "Punk ain't dead as a feeling but it's lost all the shock. To survive it needs new energy and new bands. It needs to break out of the ghetto it's trapped in. We need fresh outrage."

"You need to get up people's hooters," Jamie concurs. The Blood have been up more hooters than rolled-up dollar bills in an Aerosmith dressing room. At their debut gig at Crayford Town Hall two years ago, under the less radio friendly moniker of Coming Blood, the lads were supporting "some 'ippy synthesiser band who were boring the shit out of people"; so the Cardinal decided to pour cider on their amp and blow it up causing £450 worth of damage.

His anti-religious tirades have horrified some audiences...his royal-bashing lyrics would give the Daily Mail editor a coronary...with any luck. And it was always thus. When I first interviewed them last year their journey to Covent Garden was a voyage of revulsion that made at least one passer-by physically retch. Seriously. They were so wretchedly drunk they'd have been drummed out of Hogarth's Gin Lane for lowering the tone. Even Halfin's face drained of suntan.

Colin who was 21 then, rolled up clutching a stolen pint of lager. He wore a battered bowler hat, DM boots splattered with vomit, a tasteless pink jacket that could have been made of J cloths and army greens.

Jamie, 23, looked more like the Anti-Nowhere League's fifth member with his bike chain necklace, cut-off denim jacket, woollen titfer and unusual bracelet made of two forks bent round his wrist Uri Geller-style.

Then there were relatively silent bassist, Muttley, a 17-year-old punk resplendent in leather jacket and pink shades, and lofty drummer Dr Wildthing, who claimed to have the mental age of two (a huge over-estimation) and who sported narrow shades, leather and straights.

They got me banned from one of my favourite boozers, and when I managed to shepherd them back to the safety of Sounds' Long Acre office they very nearly got themselves banned from the building because Eric their roadie was too legless to realise that he should have been pulling the entrance door rather than pushing it and had tried to kick his way through one of the strengthened glass panels. Within minutes of arriving they were gobbing in each other's eyes and emptying ashtrays over each other's hair – and that hadn't happened in the Sounds office since that time the Nolan Sisters came to visit.

I steered them into our conference room where they defined themselves as being "all about getting pissed" and/or "taking the piss out of everybody, especially our mates our mates who've got 93 kids and two Morris Marinas, one with a vinyl roof."

They said they loved the Rejects and The Damned but hated The Jam, JJ branding Weller "a poser – he says he don't wanna be rich, gets up in the morning and falls over a wad of tenners. It's like all these boring punk bands now, there are too many cunts preaching."

As if to physically demonstrate their disgust, Col and Wildthing then started hurling things at each other, showering the unfortunate Muttley in debris and gratuitous gob. Col smashed his pint glass on the table and started to bellow loudly. I found myself suddenly sympathising with the Woolwich cops who banned their Thames Poly gig in conjunction with the college authorities on the basis of their name and reputation alone.

Their demented display approximated the sound these foul rapscallions spew out. Such Fun on the new Oi album is typical, a red-hot mix of sore throat vocals, crazed guitar and singalong supersonics. They're not an Oi band though. They're wider, wilder, and far drunker. If this band were sticks of rock they'd have the words culprit or convict written right through them. They make the Test-Tube Babies look like the Temperance Society. Wildthing, who has recently left, once demolished a drum kit with an axe.

"We're for anyone who wants to jump about and spew up," Colin explained poetically which is the closest he got to a Blood mission statement. JJ insisted they're going to "stand out like Errol Flynn's prick at an orgy" and they definitely could have done if they'd knuckled down and played more, because unlike all this beery subhuman badinage their music spoke volumes.

We talked about punk, sulphate and Tequila for a while and then we ran out of booze. "Sod this," snapped Colin. "I'm going home to nut me old gel." Then he hurled a cup of old coffee over Muttley and led the exodus to a notorious drinking den in Denmark Street frequented largely by villains and rockers. I never saw the bill for cleaning the Sounds conference room but it was sent, sarcastically I think, to the Blood via their Charlton Village local, the White Swan. I don't believe for one moment that it was ever paid.

Coming up in the Volume Three: The Clash, The Stranglers, Dexys, Ian Dury, The Skids, The Undertones, X Ray Spex, Jello Biafra, the Buzzcocks, Blitz, Siouxsie & The Banshees, Steel Pulse, Cock Sparrer, Henry Rollins, Bob Geldof, The 4-Skins, Bez, The Beat, Billy Idol, the Members and the Purple Hearts.

And in Volume Four: Saxon, Meatloaf, AC/DC, Venom, Tank, WASP, Alice Cooper, Randy Rhodes, Girlschool, Waysted, Dennis Stratton, Thunder/Terraplane, Quiet Riot, Blackmayne, Dumpy's Rusty Nuts and many more.

*And look out for Funny Guys – my adventures with the biggest names in comedy, coming soon.

About the Author

GARRY Bushell is best known for his hard-hitting, award-winning newspaper columns which have been published in the national press for 29 years. But before that he wrote for rock weekly Sounds where he covered and discovered hundreds of bands.

A fireman's son from Woolwich, south east London, Garry did his journalist training under Paul Foot on the Socialist Worker before joining the rock press in 1978.

He was the first to write about such legendary bands as the Specials, U2, Bad Manners, Secret Affair and Twisted Sister. He wrote Iron Maiden's authorised biography Running Free and co-wrote Ozzy Osbourne's first authorised biography, Diary Of A Madman. He managed the Cockney Rejects and The Blood. He fronted (and still fronts) his own band, and notched up a Number One single with the all-star charity record Let It Be – a project he conceived and organised.

Garry's Bushell On The Box TV column has appeared in The Sun, The Daily Star and The People. His own TV show of the same name Box ran for two series on ITV, attracting more than one million viewers at midnight and attaining an audience share high of 68per cent. He has appeared on more than 2,000 other TV shows, including some of television's biggest prime time hits; and many radio shows.

Garry is an outspoken broadcaster who has written novels, appeared in gangster movies and featured prominently in the acclaimed documentary films East End Babylon, Casuals and Rough Cut & Ready Dubbed. He has worked with and befriended legends of British comedy, including Benny Hill, Bob Monkhouse, Bradley Walsh, Joe Pasquale, Bobby Davro and Jim Davidson. Harry Hill has said his TV Burp was inspired by Garry's column; guests on his TV series included Lilly Savage, Vic & Bob, Craig Charles and Penn & Teller.

He has campaigned consistently for TV talent shows (when executives insisted the format was dead) and for variety shows.

Garry's column is currently published weekly in the Daily Star Sunday.

Television (as self)

Garry has appeared on more than 2,000 shows including Noel's House Party (17 appearances), The Generation Game (seven appearances), You Bet (six appearances), Celebrity Squares (five appearances), Drop The Celebrity, I'm Famous & Frightened, An Audience with Freddie Starr, the Big Big Talent Show (resident judge for the entire second series), Through The Keyhole (twelve appearances), Children In Need, Newsnight, Barrymore, the Southbank Show, The Mrs. Merton Show, The Weakest Link Celebrity Special (twice), This Morning, TVam, GMTV (resident TV critic for four months), The Big Breakfast (resident TV pundit 2001-2002), Des O'Connor Tonight, Today with Des & Mel, Celebrity Poker, Sky Poker, Showbiz Blackjack, The Wogan Show, Do The Right Thing, Hit The Road, Celebrity 15 – 1, Britain's Best Celebrity Dish, The One Show (four appearances), Loose Women (four appearances), Pets Win Prizes, Public Opinion, Stupid Punts, Saturday Night, and Nuts TV (resident pundit for six months, 2007).

Presenting: Bushell On The Box (host and writer, ITV, fifty consecutive shows), The National Alf (host and co-writer, Channel 4 documentary), Gagging For It (host and writer, ITV stand-up broadcast pilot), Garry Bushell Reveals All (quiz show host and writer, Granada M&M; four series), Sky TV talent show pilot (1996, host and writer).

Television (Acting)

Operation Good Guys (as self)
Generation Game (Sherriff of Nottingham)
Bushell On The Box (numerous parts)
Hale & Pace (Viking marauder)
Hypnotic World of Paul McKenna (randy milkman)

Journalism

Bushell On The Box began in 1987 and has appeared in The Sun, The Daily Star, The People and The Daily Star Sunday.
Walk Tall With Bushell, ran in the Star from 1991-2; a similar current affairs column ran in The Sun throughout 1994.
Garry joined the staff of the UK rock weekly Sounds in 1978, and started shifting on Fleet Street in 1985 (Sun, Daily Mirror, London Evening Standard). His writing has also appeared in Kerrang, the Independent, Vive Le Rock, Auto Express, Classic Rock, Iron Fist, Big Cheese, Temporary Hoarding, Street Sounds (launch editor and contributor) and the Modern Review.

Testimonials

Bob Monkhouse called Garry "a terrific writer, the sharpest and most knowledgeable TV critic in Britain" adding "I am proud to call him my friend."
Richard Littlejohn describes him as "the best one-liner merchant in Fleet Street."
Barbara Windsor dubbed him "the sharpest TV critic in the business."
Roy Hudd called him "the Max Miller of Fleet Street."
Former Sun editor Kelvin MacKenzie said: "He is simply the best."
Former Sun editor Stuart Higgins said: "Garry is untouched and unbeatable."
Former Sun deputy editor Fergus Shanahan said: "Outstanding, a genius."
Former People editor Neil Wallis: "Brilliantly funny, our greatest ever TV writer."

Howard Stern: "Garry Bushell is my ambassador in England."

Radio

Radio Litopia (as host); The Garry Bushell Talk Show – http://litopia.com/shows/the-garry-bushell-show/ and The Hungry & The Hunted – http://litopia.com/shows/hungry/ (2014 – 2016)
Total Rock (as DJ, 2002 – 2012)
Bloodstock Radio (as DJ, 2013)
TalkSport (as host, 2006)
Virgin Radio (as resident pundit, the Russ & Jonno Show, 1994)
Capital Gold stand-in breakfast host (2002). Numerous other radio appearances, including the Jonathan Ross Show, Steve Wright In The Afternoon, Radio One Breakfast Show, Chris Evans Drivetime, Nick Ferrari's LBC show, the Danny Baker Show etc

CPSIA information can be obtained
at www.ICGtesting.com
Printed in the USA
s0832301116

8BV00011B/106/P